Contents

Intro
duction

Welcome to the World of Custom Sneakers! A World That Elevates Sneakers to Works of Art.

Custom Sneakers: Lessons from Japan

NIKE, adidas, and other well-known brands have developed sneakers that continue to influence culture outside the confines of sport. Fans who take their love of sneakers to the extreme end up customizing regular sneakers—purchased on the open market—and turning them into rare, one-of-a-kind works of art. The culture of customizing sneakers was born in North America, and shoes by the custom sneaker brand "The Shoe Surgeon" were so popular that they sold out as soon as they went on sale, even for the incredible price of $20,000.

In Japan, there are also legendary custom sneakers that moved sports manufacturers, and this book introduces you to their work and techniques. For example, the shoe brand Hender Scheme, which originated in Asakusa, traditionally a town of shoemakers, uses high-quality leather and leather shoemaking methods to reconstruct the details of popular sneakers. Their creations have greatly

inspired sportswear brands, and in 2017 they started an official collaboration line called "adidas Originals by Hender Scheme." The "HS ZX 500 RM FL" introduced here is one of the collaboration lines released in 2018. The upper is made of high-quality leather that exudes top-quality craftsmanship, and the sole is equipped with adidas' iconic "Boost" cushioning technology.

This book covers several Japanese customizers and introduces you to their construction techniques so that you can try and enjoy them. The technical level of customization ranges from easy projects, which can be completed in a weekend, to full upper customization that requires the same skills and tools as a shoemaker. If you are inspired by this book, we hope you'll enjoy customizing your own sneakers. You just might be the one to introduce everyone to new custom sneakers that will change the world.

CASE STUDY
#01
ANGELUS PAINT

ANGELUS PAINT >>
JUNKYARD

The Most Popular Sneaker Paint:
What You Need to Know about Angelus Paint

Angelus Paint is by far the most well known and popular paint for sneakers. It is a water-based acrylic paint with excellent concealment properties. It has obtained the greatest market share in the United States—the home of custom sneakers. Of course, many Japanese custom builders are also Angelus Paint enthusiasts, and it often appears in the projects introduced here. The following is a selection of Angelus Paint variations and related products. Before jumping into actual customization cases, let's go through some basic knowledge regarding sneaker-specific paints.

In Cooperation With: JUNKYARD

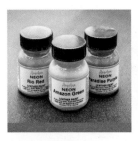

Standard Paints

These are the basic colors. There are about eighty variations to date. Of course, it's also possible to mix and match to create original colors.

Neon Paints

Variations of Angelus Paint that produce vivid neon colors. There are a total of twelve colors in the lineup, including vivid yellow and green.

Metallic

Metallic colors can be used to create a "dazzling" look. In addition to standard metallic colors, like gold and silver, there is also a bronze variation that provides an aged look.

Pearlescent Paints

Available in seven colors, pearlescent paint can produce a unique glossy finish. As with the standard paints, these can also be mixed.

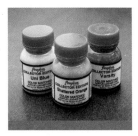

Collector Edition

These color variations are inspired by colors used in popular sneakers. These are excellent products to rely on when trying to match your custom kicks with your favorite sneakers.

Glitter Paints

This is a variation of transparent paint with glitter added. This allows for the expression of accents, while making the most of the base color. Also used for nail art.

Acrylic Finisher

Finisher used as a topcoat after paint has dried. There are different variations of surface gloss, with Matte being the most lusterless.

2-Thin

A thinner that is suitable for Angelus Paint. Can be added to paint that has become too thick while in storage, or to adjust density for airbrushing.

Leather Preparer and Deglazer

Deglazer is a solvent used to pretreat surfaces for paint. Removes coating from commercial sneakers and improves paint adhesion.

Scratch-Resistant Sealer

A durable topcoat often used in combination with Angelus Paint. Commonly referred to as "Scratch Sealer."

CASE STUDY
#02
ONE-POINT PAINTING

ONE-POINT PAINTING >>
NIKE BY YOU AIR MAX 90

Applying One-Point Painting to
Official Custom Sneakers Completes the Look

Sneakers created by manufacturers' official customization services are among the most familiar to sneaker fans. However, there's a limit to the number of options available because the color of the custom parts is restricted by the website. The "NIKE By You" service provided by NIKE (formerly NIKEiD) is difficult to use and is often ridiculed on social-networking sites as a service that "can't scratch the itch." But as you will see, it is possible to improve NIKE By You quality with a simple paint job.

In Cooperation with JUNKYARD Koenji, Sneakers at Random Koenji

Major Skills Acquired

Start
CUSTOMIZATION SKILL

Confirming Area to Be Painted
Selecting the Right Paint for the Material

This is an official customization service, provided by manufacturers, where you can choose from preset colors and materials on the web and receive your own sneakers in a few weeks. NIKE By You is the most popular official customization service, with many users. In this section, we will introduce an easy and effective way to upgrade NIKE By You service sneakers based on the Air Max 90, released in February 2020.

01 This NIKE By You customization uses one of NIKE's most classic sneakers—the Air Max 90—as its base. In addition to the standard color scheme, special monotone materials could be selected for this limited-time item. Our project also incorporates a mosaic-like graphic part on the mudguard and quarter.

02 It may seem strange for custom-ordered sneakers to be available for only a limited time, but providing limited editions is actually a common NIKE practice to encourage people to buy their products. Not surprisingly, NIKE By You items frequently followed this policy. For users who prefer NIKE By You products, it's not uncommon for limited-edition parts to be sold out before users can even choose their parts.

03 Overall satisfaction with the NIKE By You Air Max 90 is high. The only dissatisfaction is the solid-colored back tab and the fact that the color of the Nike Air branding cannot be changed like the commercial models. This kind of "itch you can't scratch" annoyance is a common negative point among official customization services, not just NIKE By You.

04 Based on the color scheme of the sneakers themselves, and the material to be painted, Angelus Paint's "Gift Box Blue" was chosen. This color is reminiscent of gift boxes used by Tiffany and is one of the standard colors used in NIKE sneakers. It is labeled as "Jade."

CUSTOMIZATION SKILL

Pretreatment of Area to be Painted
Proper Pretreatment of Target Material Is Paramount

The term "custom-painted sneakers" evokes images of painted leather or canvas materials, but for the Air Max 90 we selected, the heel portion is our target. The problem is that the custom base is made of TPU (thermoplastic polyurethane).

To apply paint to a synthetic resin like this, it is important to first rough up the surface with sandpaper to improve adhesion. By contrast, pretreatment of leather removes oil from the target surface.

01 Although general sandpaper is sufficient to rough up the TPU, sponge abrasives with excellent flexibility will make the work go smoother. If the purpose is to improve paint adhesion, it is generally recommended to use sanding sponges with a grit between 320 and 400.

02 In this case, the target area is not the entire section of TPU but rather the Swoosh and the "NIKE AIR" printing. A sanding sponge with firm corners will make it easier to "sand" small areas, like the logo. Rather than simply scraping the surface of the target area, it is better to remove a thin layer of "skin." Sand until the gloss becomes dull.

03 After sanding the areas to be painted, use a brush to remove any loose shavings. Then, clean with acetone. This process is necessary to remove invisible dust, but acetone can damage the TPU material itself. So, it is really important to work quickly and use the smallest amount of acetone possible.

04 TPU material after pretreatment, but before painting. In this case, we sanded the unpainted TPU to help the paint stick. However, if you are repainting previously painted TPU, you can just wipe with acetone to remove surface oil.

>>

CUSTOMIZATION SKILL

Custom Paint Color Coordination
Color Matching Makes a Big Difference in the Final Product

We begin by using Angelus Paint to color the Swoosh on the heel. The Angelus brand doesn't just have basic colors; there are also specialty colors inspired by popular sneakers. However, in many cases the colors are slightly different, even if they are based on popular colors. In order to improve consistency, it is best to actually try out the paint and compare coloration after it has dried. Then make adjustments for a more well-matched look.

05 Water-based acrylic paints like Angelus harden when exposed to air, so it is important to separate them on a palette specifically made for watercolors, or models, when applying a test coat. The key to long-lasting paint is to keep the lid closed and stir to keep as much air as possible out of the paint that remains inside the bottle.

06 The customizer had sneakers available for test painting in this case, so he could check the finish. If you wanted to check the color yourself, you could just use paper. However, I recommend using leather scraps or buying a cheap synthetic leather bag from a secondhand store. That way you can check the texture as well.

07 After the paint has dried thoroughly, compare the blue tone from the Swoosh with your sample. It is difficult to tell from the image, but the Angelus Paint produced a slightly darker color. Although it would not look out of place if painted as is, we decided to take all possible precautions and adjust the color.

08 To lighten the tone here, we added "Flat White" from Angelus Paint. "Flat" paints in the Angelus line have a matte finish. Although the final shine will be adjusted when the topcoat is applied, it is best to use a paint that has been designed with the finished product in mind so you can visualize the finished texture.

Custom Paint Color Coordination
Using Additives Compatible with Chosen Materials

CUSTOMIZATION SKILL

Unlike with plastic models, there is no detailed color-mixing recipe for custom sneakers. In order to achieve the desired color, even professionals need to make minor adjustments. In addition, Angelus Paint has additives for various materials.

Additives affect paint adherence and strength after it has dried, so it is a good idea to use them, even when painting a single small area.

09 Mix paints transferred to the palette to achieve target color. Since there is no exact recipe, the basic rule is to first mix by eye and then make fine adjustments. However, if you are using an airbrush, you can add the optional thinner, "Angelus 2-Thin," to adjust thinness of the paint.

10 Try out the color-matched paint at several stages in order to get closer to the target, while still compensating for the missing color. It is also important to dry the paint thoroughly before checking, since the color may change after drying. In this case, a heat gun can be used for quick drying, thereby increasing efficiency.

11 In this case, we were able to create the target color after just two recalibrations. It would certainly take more time and effort to create this type of intermediate color if we had started with a primary color. In this sense, Angelus Paint, with its lineup of popular sneaker colors, can help sneaker customizers by reducing time and effort.

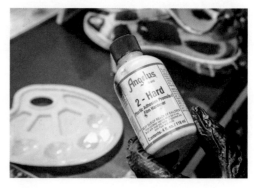

12 Add an appropriate amount of "Angelus 2-Hard" (sold separately) to the finished paint. This is an additive used to paint hard materials, such as TPU and other plastics, that are used in sneakers. On the other hand, for softer parts such as the mesh material of the tongue, the idea is to use an additive called "Angelus 2-Soft."

>>

Partial Painting of Sneaker Parts and Brush Selection

Applying Thin Layers Improves Finish Accuracy

Once the surface has been prepped and the paint mixed, it is time to color. It's important not to apply too much paint at any one time. Angelus Paints hide underlying colors better than ordinary water-based acrylic, so it is tempting to apply a single coat. But applying one thick coat is risky since it can lead to running. That being said, basic principles of painting with thin layers should be faithfully followed.

13 It is important to prepare a variety of brushes. You could always purchase brushes at a dollar store, but most of them will have stiff bristles that make it difficult to apply the correct amount of pressure. It is best to use high-quality, hobbyist or professional, brushes in order to have greater flexibility while painting.

14 Use a fine-tip brush and paint carefully when doing fine details. The first coat of paint may be a little uneven, but don't worry about it. Also, if you are not confident in your painting skills, it's a good idea to apply masking tape around the target areas.

15 Once the first coat is complete, use a heat gun to dry. Shortening the drying time not only increases efficiency but also reduces the risk of dust sticking to the surface before drying. If you don't have a heat gun, you can use a hairdryer instead, but a heat gun has higher temperatures and is much easier to use on DIY projects.

16 Once the first coat is dry, go ahead an apply the second coat. Despite the dark black base color, the bright jade appears quite vivid thanks to the excellent concealing properties of Angelus Paint. A small amount of overflow can be easily fixed with acetone, so don't be afraid to make mistakes.

>>

CUSTOMIZATION SKILL

Topcoating of Painted Surfaces
Ensures Durability

The next step is to apply a topcoat, often called a finisher or sealer, to the painted surface. The main purpose of the topcoat is to ensure durability when worn and to make the surface shine. In this case, for the final step we used Raleigh Restoration's "Scratch Resistant Sealer," which is highly trusted by sneaker customization experts.

17 Topcoating with Raleigh Restoration's Scratch Resistant Sealer will significantly increase the durability of the painted surface, but it also makes it much more difficult to correct any runs in the paint. Before topcoating, check the painted surface again and use sandpaper or acetone to correct any areas that need to be fixed.

18 After making sure the surface is completely dry, apply the Scratch Resistant Sealer, using a brush. The liquid Scratch Resistant Sealer is cloudy white, but don't worry— it dries to a colorless transparent finish. It will still be possible to repaint with Angelus Paint or other paints after the topcoat treatment, so don't worry if you don't like the color.

19 The topcoat affects the overall strength of the painted surface, so don't forget to apply it. The Scratch Resistant Sealer we used this time produces a matte finish. If you want to change to a glossy finish, just recoat the surface with Angelus Paint's "High Gloss Acrylic Finisher" after the Scratch Resistant Sealer has dried.

20 Once the topcoat on one shoe is complete, it is best to dry it with a heat gun before moving on to the other shoe. As with painting, shortening topcoat dry time also protects the painted surface from dust. It is no exaggeration to say that a heat gun is an essential item when custom-painting sneakers.

>>

One-Point Painting Completion
Just Change Part Colors to Upgrade the Look and Feel

The one-point paint job based on NIKE's official customization service NIKE By You, introduced here, was done by a professional. It took less than an hour to complete both shoes. If you are an inexperienced customizer, you may need more time, but once you have the necessary tools, it is easy enough to do as a weekend DIY project. Angelus Paint, which has a lineup of paints reminiscent of the colors of popular sneakers, is sure to help make such "weekend DIY" projects much easier.

CUSTOMIZER INFORMATION

3-53-8 Koenji-Minami, Suginami-ku, Tokyo, Japan 166-0003
Phone: 03-5913-7690
Junkyard Koenji
Sneakers at
Random Koenji Store

https://sneaker-at-random.com/

Store Manager
Mr. Yamaguchi

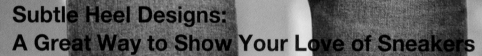

Subtle Heel Designs:
A Great Way to Show Your Love of Sneakers

ONE-POINT PAINTING
NIKE BY YOU AIR MAX 90

CASE STUDY
#03
WATERSLIDE DECAL PAPER CUSTOMIZATION

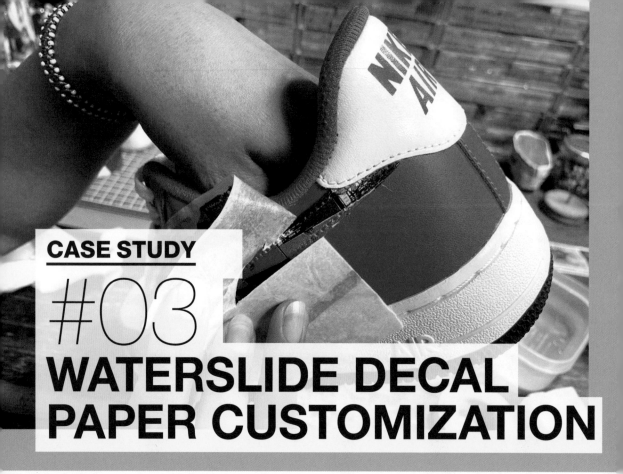

CASE STUDY
#03
WATERSLIDE DECAL PAPER CUSTOMIZATION

WATERSLIDE DECAL PAPER CUSTOMIZATION >>
NIKE AIR FORCE 1 LOW

Using My Pride and Joy Sneaker Collection in My Designs: Easy Customization that Can Be Completed Quickly

The hydro dip technique for transferring film stencils onto sneakers, as seen on YouTube, can reproduce graphics that are difficult to draw by hand. However, the hydrographic film used is difficult to obtain, and only limited graphical designs are available. I came up with the idea of "waterslide decal paper customization" to make it easier to customize sneakers while keeping the fun alive. Let's try customizing sneakers, in a way that only sneaker collectors can, with just a home printer and waterslide decal transfer paper.

Production: CUSTOMIZE KICKS MAGAZINE Editorial Department

Start

CUSTOMIZATION SKILL

Preparing Waterslide Decal Paper
Don't Forget to Flip the Design before Printing

In order to re-create a custom "WE LOVE NIKE" style of sneaker design, from my own collection, this customization used home-printer-compatible waterslide decal paper. Although waterslide decal papers have the disadvantage of not being able to reproduce original colors—unless used on a white background—they are very easy to use and reasonably priced. This makes them suitable for beginners. There is no reason not to take advantage of these materials.

01 Waterslide decal paper uses an inkjet printer to add patterns to a transparent sheet. If the surface where the sheet will be applied isn't white, the color cannot be properly reproduced. If you want to reproduce the actual printed color, you need to choose a white surface on the sneaker, or paint it white beforehand.

02 The product used here is a PLUS brand "Inkjet Waterslide Decal Paper." It can be easily purchased on Amazon as an import for around $30 for a pack of three sheets (other options are available). Some product reviews mention that the transferred graphics are easily washed off, but this is not a problem if you take the provided waterproofing measures.

03 The image used for the decal film was a pile of boxed sneakers, from the 1990s, lined up in my sneaker collection room. You can see that there were also NIKE reproduction boxes from that era. I arranged them in a haphazard manner and took pictures with my smartphone instead of a single-lens reflex camera.

04 Waterslide decal paper is designed to have the decal film directly attached to the target, meaning the design is reversed left to right. Therefore, when printing on your PC, be sure to reverse the left and right sides of the image digitally. Here, I made one version with the image I took as is, and also two horizontal versions with multiple copied images side by side.

CUSTOMIZATION SKILL

Surface Preparation for Design Transfer

Surface Preparation at the Level of a Professional Customization Store

This customization process doesn't involve paint or brushes. It mainly involves attaching the decal film to the target areas. The process itself is very easy and quick, but it is useless if the transferred graphics are easily peeled off. In order to avoid this, it is important to prepare a good base. We will go through the same level of pretreatment as we would when custom painting.

05 In this example, the waterslide decal paper will be applied only to the side panel Swooshes. A strong solvent such as acetone is used for the pretreatment. In addition to preparing the design for the waterslide decal paper, the area around the Swoosh should be carefully masked to protect it.

06 Here, masking tape has been applied all the way around the Swoosh. This time, instead of applying the tape neatly around the Swoosh, tape off a wide area and then cut out the Swoosh with a precision knife. Either way, as long as the tape is applied properly, there is no problem.

07 Wipe the Swoosh surface—wherever the waterslide decal paper will be applied—with acetone to remove the factory finish and any oils present. Prepare acetone from a home improvement store, a plastic dispenser with a pump, and a melamine sponge from a dollar store. This surface prep is the same as for any professional.

08 Transfer some acetone from the can to the pump dispenser, using a dropper. Dispense acetone onto sponge and clean the Swoosh surface. When cleaning white areas, it is often difficult to see the paint itself come off. However, you may notice paint on your fingers or gloves. Just remember to clean the surface well while keeping the image of peeling off a thin layer of paint in mind.

Primer Application and Waterslide Decal Paper Preparation

CUSTOMIZATION SKILL

The Goal Is to Create the Effect of Stacked Boxes on the Swooshes

Apply primer to the surface of the Swoosh after cleaning with acetone. As of this writing, there is no primer on the market that is specifically designed for custom sneaker painting (there are primers for adhesives).

09 Raleigh Restoration's Scratch Resistant Sealer, commonly known as "Scratch Sealer," is a favorite topcoat for many customizers. It is used not only as a topcoat, but also as a primer because of its strong adhesion to both the materials and painted surfaces of sneakers.

10 Brush undiluted Scratch Sealer onto the Swoosh. Scratch Sealer can be used as a base coat, and since it is water-based, it can be adjusted by adding water if it is too thick. Moreover, the brushes used can be easily cleaned with water. It may not be affordable, but its ease of use is very appealing.

11 Check the design balance of the waterslide decal paper that will be applied to the Swoosh. If the pattern is too large, the boxes won't really appear to be stacked. If it is too small, the desired "sneaker box" look will disappear. Here, we selected the version with two side-by-side images. It will be applied to the Swoosh.

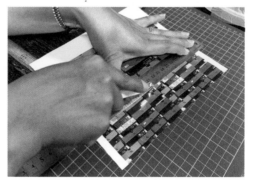

12 After confirming the overall balance of the design, cut out the portion of the waterslide decal paper you want to use. Use a cutting mat and stainless-steel ruler to cut straight lines. In the end, waterslide decal paper will be applied to all four Swooshes, two on each side, but we decided to complete one part first as a quality check.

CUSTOMIZATION SKILL

How to Apply Waterslide Decal Paper
Soak Surface with Water to Prevent Air Bubbles

After creating the base, and confirming the balance of the design to be expressed on the Swoosh, let's actually apply the waterslide decal paper. Place the printed side on the Swoosh and apply water to the backside (as shown). This nostalgic process is similar to water-transferring of stickers on plastic models. As long as you haven't applied any finisher, the sheet can be peeled off, so don't be afraid to make mistakes.

13 To apply the waterslide decal paper, all you need is a sponge and water. This ease of application is sure to be attractive to customization beginners. The decal film will begin to peel at the slightest touch of water, so be careful not to let any water droplets splash onto the paper until you get it in place.

14 Place the waterslide decal paper with the printed side on the Swoosh and, after confirming its position, fix with masking tape. After reconfirming the position, moisten the backing paper with water so that the decal sticks. Careful: if you fix both ends of the paper before applying water to the middle, the design will wrinkle. So, it is important to first fix one side of the paper before wetting it, and then moving away from that fixed end.

15 Here, the entire waterslide decal paper has been covered with water and is now adhered to the sneaker. If any air bubbles appear between the paper and the Swoosh, use a moist sponge to force them out. The backing paper absorbs water surprisingly well, so don't forget to moisten the sponge frequently.

16 Once the water has penetrated the entire waterslide decal paper, peel off the backing paper. Be sure to peel it before the decal paper dries. If the decal paper is well soaked with water, the backing should peel off easily. Can you see that the design, which was reversed on the decal film, has been transferred to the Swoosh in its original state?

>>

Masking Tape Removal
Remove Masking Tape before the Decal Film Is Completely Dry

After removing the backing from the waterslide decal paper, the masking tape around the Swoosh needs to be removed. Since the base color of the Air Force 1 is orange, I tried to use orange as the main color for the design on the Swoosh. If the design doesn't turn out the way you want, you can simply peel off the decals and start the process over again.

17 Here, the waterslide decal paper backing has been completely removed. Initially I wondered whether I should remove the masking tape before or after the decals dried. However, given that the manufacturer recommends removal while wet, I decided to take the tape off before the decals were completely dry. This is also similar to the way water transfer stickers work on plastic models.

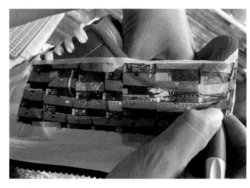

18 Before removing the masking tape, I used a precision knife to lightly trace along the detail of the Swoosh, just to be safe. I didn't try to "cut" the attached sheet; I just applied a bit of force to score the tape. Although it is difficult to verify how effectively you are scoring the tape until you are finished, it is important to remember that a "do what you can" attitude is essential for DIY.

19 Peel the masking tape off slowly from the rear end of the Swoosh. This is a tense moment, since you can now check how well your work has gone. In this example, the work is progressing smoothly, but if there are any areas where the transferred image is peeling along the tape, use a precision knife to cut the tape off or make other recovery attempts.

20 All the masking tape has been removed from around the Swoosh. You can see that the image of the stacked-up boxes is reproduced beautifully. The result is so good that you can't help but feel proud of yourself. Once you are satisfied with the finish of the design, let it dry thoroughly and then apply the topcoat to the Swoosh.

CUSTOMIZATION SKILL

Topcoating Transferred Designs
Two Layers Will Protect the Transferred Design from Water

The waterslide decal paper will peel off when wet, so we need to coat it. Don't just coat the surface of the Swoosh; you also need to coat the edges. It would be easy to use a clear urethane-based paint, also used by professionals, but these paints contain harmful ingredients and require a suitable painting environment. Use urethane paint only if you have the correct work environment.

21 Two layers of topcoat are applied. The first coat is Raleigh Restoration's Scratch Sealer, which was also used as a primer. Touch the Swoosh with your finger to make sure the decals are dry, then use a brush to apply Scratch Sealer to the entire Swoosh.

22 The main point in this process is to apply the topcoat to the edges of the Swoosh, in addition to the face. It is important to apply the topcoat to the cross section without leaving any residue, just as you did with the side panels.

23 Urethane-based finishers contain harmful ingredients and are difficult to handle, so we will use Angelus Acrylic Finisher as our second topcoat. Apply a single layer of Acrylic Finisher over Scratch Sealer. It is not expected to be waterproof, but it will make the entire surface shine and produce a beautiful finish.

24 The Acrylic Finisher should be carefully applied to the edges of the Swooshes, in the same manner as the Scratch Sealer. After coating the transferred image with your two layers of topcoat, the customization is complete. If you want to add more water resistance, you can spray on some sneaker-waterproofing agent.

>>

Complete
CUSTOMIZATION SKILL

Completed Waterslide Decal Paper Customization
Easy Customization That Can Be Completed in a Single Weekend

Repeat the process of applying waterslide decal paper to all of the other Swooshes, and you're done! When editorial staff members worked on this project at home, it took them about three hours to complete both shoes. Even though this is a comparatively short amount of time for a sneaker customization, the results are very reminiscent of the "WE LOVE NIKE" customization by Atmos, released in 2018 (a NIKE/Atmos collab available in Japan). Since this customization is made by just transferring your own images or photos, it is a skill

that can be applied to a variety of shoe designs, like the Air Jordan 1. As for water resistance, which I was worried about, it seems that the decals won't come off if they just get sprinkled with water, like from a shower. However, if you actually wear the sneakers, the design might get wrinkled, and the decals may come off when water seeps under them. If you want to enjoy your completed custom sneakers for a long time, just check the weather forecast and avoid wearing them on rainy days.

Produced by
CUSTOMIZE KICKS MAGAZINE
Editorial Department

Customization Styles
That Help Your Collection Take Shape
WATERSLIDE DECAL PAPER CUSTOMIZATION
NIKE AIR FORCE 1 LOW

CASE STUDY
#04
STENCIL PAINTING

CASE STUDY
#04
STENCIL PAINTING

CASE STUDY #04

STENCIL PAINTING >>
NIKE ×TRAVIS SCOTT AIR MAX 270 "CACTUS TRAILS"

Manufacturer-Recommended Custom Painting with Stencil Airbrushing

Custom sneakers are basically a hobby, enjoyed by those who are not satisfied with manufacturers' products. That being said, there are certain sneakers that are actually officially recommended for customization by the manufacturer. The Air Max 270, introduced here and created in collaboration with Travis Scott, is one of the sneakers officially recommended for custom painting. Here, we will introduce the process of painting a vivid "Reverse Swoosh" on the Air Max 270 upper by reproducing the procedures recommended by the manufacturer.

In Cooperation with Creator's One: Monozukuri Working Space

Start

CUSTOMIZATION SKILL

Stencil Sheet Preparation
Cutout Accuracy Will Affect Finished Product

The official stencil to apply the Swoosh to a pair of NIKE ×Travis Scott Air Max 270 "CACTUS TRAILS" released in 2020, was used here. Stenciling is a technique for transferring letters and/or illustrations, using a template. Stencil data for this particular customization used to be available for download on the official website, but it has been taken down. So, you will have to make your own stencil by copying the side panel of an existing sneaker or downloading a stencil off the internet.

01 This time, the stenciled Swoosh was airbrushed onto the Air Max 270. Interestingly, the kids' model of the Travis Scott collaboration model had an orange Swoosh on the upper, but this men's shoe has only a small Swoosh on the front and back. In order to re-create the same look as the kids' model, you will need to airbrush the Swoosh yourself.

02 Use a printer to print off a Swoosh stencil, downloaded from the official website, onto sticker paper. If you don't have any experience with stencils, you may want to print it out on regular paper before printing it on sticker paper, in order to practice cutting out the Swoosh.

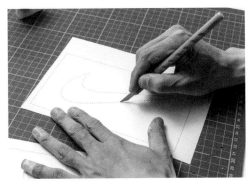

03 Cut printed sticker paper for both the left and right shoe. Use a precision knife to cut out Swoosh details as if you were tracing along a dotted line. Don't forget to keep the stencil interiors you cut out, since you will use them for positioning in a later step.

04 Left and right Swoosh details cut out on the sticker paper. The shape you cut out here will be reflected on the sneaker, so it is important to be precise. In this case, the stencil is stuck to the sneaker like a sticker. Then, the cutout portion is painted with an airbrush, so the stencil is basically disposable.

CUSTOMIZATION SKILL

Adjusting Stencil Position

Add Reverse Swoosh to Left and Right Outside Edge

The Swoosh on the kids' model is opposite to the normal one and is most often called the "Reverse Swoosh." With that background out of the way, let's add the Reverse Swoosh to the men's model. This is where the stencil pattern "scraps" come in handy. Use these scraps to adjust the position of the Reverse Swoosh and create your ideal custom sneaker.

05 Here is the stencil and the cutout Swoosh from the previous step. Although the official data for the Air Max 270 stencil has been released, there is no diagram for the Swoosh placement. Placement of the Swoosh is left up to the customizer's personal taste.

06 A piece of sticker paper, cut out in the shape of a Swoosh, can be attached to the sneaker's upper by peeling off the backing. However, since you will have to reapply the sticker many times before you get it in the right position, it would be easier to use small pieces of masking tape to just hold the cutout Swoosh piece in place.

07 After examining the position of the Swoosh, we choose a balanced position that flows from front to back, with part of it protruding down into the midsole. In this position, we will have to paint parts made of different materials. This shouldn't be a problem if we do the proper groundwork and prioritize the "coolness" of the customization.

08 The other shoe masked up. The plan is to paint the Swoosh the same bright-orange color as the Kids' model, which means it will probably be a very prominent detail when finished. For this reason, we need to try to make it as symmetrical as possible, so it won't look out of place.

>>

Attaching Stencil
It Is Difficult to Apply Paper Stencil to Curved Surfaces

Once you have decided on the Swoosh position, you can use the temporarily fixed scrap parts as a guide and attach the stencil. At this point, make cuts in the sticker backing material so it can be peeled off in sections from the rear half and front half of the stencil. If the stencil is not in the correct position, the painted Swoosh will also be out of place. Proceed with caution to ensure symmetry.

09 Set the stencil in the correct position, with the hole in the stencil overlying the temporarily attached Swoosh cutout. Once you have adjusted the sticker position, peel backing paper from rear half and attach it to the upper. This portion of the sticker will be pressed down in a later step, so it is acceptable to just place the stencil in the correct position here.

10 After the rear half of the stencil is attached to the upper and lightly fixed in position, lift up the front half of the stencil and remove the scrap Swoosh that was used as a guideline while mounting. Be sure to remove the masking tape that held the scrap Swoosh in place, since the entire stencil will be attached to the upper in the following process.

11 Now peel off the backing paper from the front half of the sticker and attach it to the upper. If there are any wrinkles in the sticker pattern, the Swoosh detail will be lost. The surface of the shoe is uneven, so it may be a bit difficult to cleanly apply the sticker. The best way to apply the pattern is to move along gradually toward the front while lightly pressing down.

12 Finish applying the stencil to the upper. The stencil sticker is made from paper, which is to say it is not very flexible. It will wrinkle slightly when applied to curved surfaces. Here, the Swoosh detail is not very distorted, so leave it as is and continue to work with it. However, as a test case, try making a stencil with flexible material for the other shoe.

>>

CASE STUDY #04

>> NIKE ×TRAVIS SCOTT AIR MAX 270 "CACTUS TRAILS"

STENCIL PAINTING

CUSTOMIZATION SKILL

CUSTOMIZATION SKILL

Attach Stencil Paper

Use Stencil Vinyl to Create Patterns and Easily Attach Them to Upper

Making patterns with sticker material is recommended by official sources. However, sticker material doesn't mold to the details of the upper very well, and we had a hard time attaching it nicely. Given this situation, the owner of Creator's

One suggested we use self-adhesive stencil vinyl (hereafter stencil vinyl) to make a pattern that would mold into the details better. So, from here on we will proceed while using stencil vinyl instead of plastic sticker material.

13 Use stencil vinyl to make your stencil. First, cut the stencil vinyl to the appropriate size. Then, attach a label sticker—with the Swoosh cut out—on the stencil vinyl, using masking tape. Cut the stencil vinyl with a precision knife along the lines of the label sticker Swoosh and you're done.

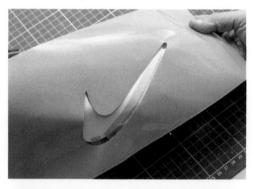

14 Match the stencil vinyl pattern to the scrap parts temporarily fixed to the upper. Check to see if there is any distortion in the Swoosh. Unlike with paper stickers, it takes a certain amount of experience to cut out thick stencil vinyl so that it appears sharp and clean. It is best to practice with scraps until you get used to it.

15 After confirming that the Swoosh detail in the stencil vinyl hasn't been distorted, cut it to a size that can be easily attached to the shoe, peel off the backing paper, and attach it to the upper. The stencil vinyl used here has no particular specifications, but you should have no problem finding popular products that are easy to obtain online or at a craft store.

16 Press the stencil vinyl into the details of the upper and remove the Swoosh-shaped scrap that was temporarily fixed in place. You can clearly see how much better it adheres to the shape when compared to the paper stencil. I'm looking forward to seeing the difference in the finished product when compared to the other shoe with the paper sticker attached.

>>

Shoe Masking
Choose Appropriate Masking Method for the Chosen Painting Style

CUSTOMIZATION SKILL

After attaching the stencil to the upper, mask off the areas that will not be painted. There are several ways to paint inside stencils, but the most common is to use an airbrush or spray can. In the example shown here, Angelus Paint will be sprayed on with an airbrush. However, I asked the customizer to use the masking method he would employ when painting with a spray can on one of the shoes.

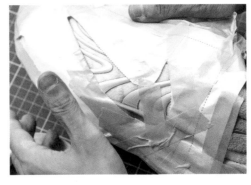

17 The first step is to mask off the shoe as if you were anticipating using an airbrush. When an airbrush is used properly, the paint will not be scattered over a very large area. So, just try to apply masking tape around the stencil area so that there are no gaps, while keeping in mind the direction of the paint spray.

18 Masked up for airbrushing. The masking tape is applied to areas where paint might splash. In the photo, masking tape has also been applied to the area to be painted, but this is just to secure the stencil edges to the upper. The plan is to paint the nonmasked areas first, then remove the tape and repaint.

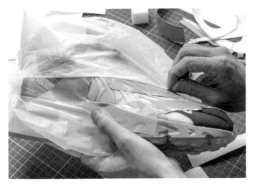

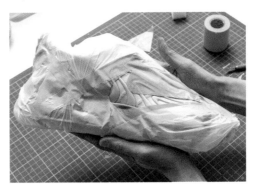

19 On the other shoe, masking tape and plastic have been applied in anticipation of painting with a spray can. Since the amount of paint in a spray can cannot be adjusted, it is necessary to move the can quickly to make sure that the paint doesn't drip. As a result, paint will be scattered over a wide area. So, the entire shoe will need to be masked.

20 The owner of Creator's One covered the sneakers with dollar store plastic bags and fixed them in position along the stencil with masking tape. In a short time, he was able to complete the masking process for everything except the target area. Using the right materials in the right places, keeping the reasons for masking in mind, and paying attention to the painting method will greatly improve efficiency.

>>

CUSTOMIZATION
SKILL

Preparing Paints and Airbrush
A Compatible Paint Thinner Is Essential for Airbrushing

After masking off the areas to be stenciled, we will paint the Swoosh. Stencils work well with airbrushing, and we can even use the same Angelus Paints as for brush-on customization. Note that there are some excellent airbrush-specific paints on the market, such as "SOMAY-Q," but they don't have as many color options. From here, I will show you how to airbrush the stencil.

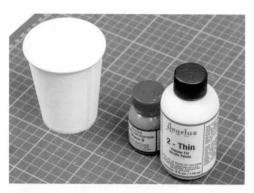

21 The color used in this example is Angelus' "Blaze 8." The orange is similar to that used in other NIKE sneakers, and Blaze 8 is one of Angelus' "Collector Edition Paints." When using Angelus Paint in an airbrush, you need to dilute it by adding about twice as much diluent as when brushing.

22 Add Angelus 2-Thin and Blaze 8—in 2:1 ratio—to a paper cup. Adjust concentrations until you find the correct viscosity level for airbrushing. If the paint is poured into the airbrush undiluted, it will form lumps and spray everywhere, so be sure to mix with the thinner in a cup first. Also, water-based acrylic paints harden when exposed to air, so be sure to close the lid after transferring the required amount to your airbrush.

23 This time, the customizer will use the airbrush that is permanently installed at the Creator's One shop to paint the Swoosh. First, crimp the rim of the paper cup and pour the adjusted Angelus Paint + thinner into the airbrush paint cup. It should be noted that it is far easier to mix the paint in the paper cup to get the desired color.

24 One trick for thoroughly agitating the paint is to first pour the mixture into the airbrush paint cup. Then, hold your finger over the nozzle and lightly press the trigger. This will cause the air to flow back up the gun and agitate whatever is in the paint cup. There are stores where you can rent equipment, and their knowledgeable staff often offer programs that teach airbrushing for a small fee. This is truly reassuring for beginners.

>>

CUSTOMIZATION SKILL

Spray On the Swoosh
Check the Condition of the Surface as You Airbrush

Once the airbrush has been made ready, we will paint the Swoosh on the upper. The stencil vinyl used in the previous step was already firmly attached to the upper, so the right foot will be painted first. Normally, we would clean the painted surface with acetone beforehand, but this upper is made of rubber, which could be seriously degraded by solvents. So, we just went ahead and cleaned the surface with alcohol-based wet wipes.

25 Lightly airbrush the edge of the Swoosh to check color and consistency. If you use acetone or primer to prepare the basecoat as you would with leather sneakers, you don't need to worry about this testing step, but since rubber is used here, you need to test paint-first.

26 Dry the thinly painted area and check the condition of the painted surface. The result here was that there were no signs of peeling or cracking. This means that there should be no problem using a topcoat after painting. This judgment was made based on the use of the appropriate paint for the sneakers. However, if you use a different type of paint, you might need to proceed more carefully.

27 The paint is airbrushed on in thin layers. The target surface is beige, which made me wonder if the Blaze 8 orange color would come out as I imagined. However, after checking the sprayed surface, I was quite pleased when there seemed to be no problem. If you use this same method for other colors, be aware that you might need to add a base color (most frequently white) so that the coloring is correct.

28 Here is the right upper with the stenciled-on Swoosh. The painting went quite well, not just on the upper but also on the midsole where the Reverse Swoosh protrudes. After this, the topcoat is applied, but before that, the painted surface must be allowed to dry thoroughly. The other shoe can be airbrushed now to take advantage of the dry time.

>>

CUSTOMIZATION SKILL

Spray On the Swoosh

Sticker Papers Are More Likely to Have Gaps Than Stencil Vinyl

Sticker paper doesn't conform to the details of the sneakers as well as the stencil vinyl, and there are gaps between the upper and stencil. Normally, the stickers would have been replaced with stencil vinyl, which adheres to the shoe more easily, but

this time the angle of the airbrush was simply adjusted to prevent paint from getting into the gaps.

29 Next, proceed to airbrush the left shoe with the sticker stencil attached. The masking tape used to hold the stencil in place has been removed because it seemed like it would interfere with the airbrushing. The area has been remasked with a plastic bag so we can concentrate on airbrushing without worrying about overspray.

30 Turn sneaker as you spray so that the smallest amount of paint possible gets between sneaker and stencil. Even if the Swoosh edge happens to blur a bit, it can still be enjoyed as a unique piece. However, we must really try not to apply the paint too haphazardly or else the end result won't be the desired, distinctive Swoosh.

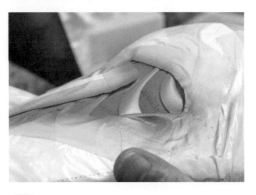

31 You can see there is a gap between the sneaker body and the stencil. The manufacturer's official recommendation was to use a sticker paper, but stencil vinyl didn't produce such large gaps. It probably depends on the surface material of the sneakers, but in this case, using stencil vinyl was probably the right choice.

32 Here we have the Swoosh stenciled on both shoes. At this point, the right Swoosh appears to be a bit higher than the left. Don't worry though; it shouldn't be noticeable. Now that we've gone this far, it is time to move on to the finishing touch: the topcoat. I hope adjusting the direction of the airbrush will be effective here as well.

>>

CUSTOMIZATION SKILL 7

Spraying Topcoat
Scratch Sealer Makes for an Easy-to-Use Airbrush Topcoat

After airbrushing the Swooshes on both shoes, I sprayed on the topcoat to finish. We used Raleigh Restoration's Scratch Sealer, which many customizers say "dramatically improves the strength of acrylic paint." Scratch Sealer dries colorless and transparent, so it Is easy to apply evenly with a brush. However, in this case, a standard airbrush was used to apply it.

33 After stenciling, the sneakers were dried in an electrical dish dryer—next to the sink—to completely dry the painted surface. It is not uncommon to see dish dryers in hobby workspaces, such as Creator's One, but the sight of sneakers in a dish dryer was quite surprising and kind of impressive, actually.

34 After the surface is completely dry, Raleigh Restoration's Scratch Sealer is applied. This Scratch Sealer dries to a matte finish, so if you want to give the painted area a glossier look, it is best to apply a second glossy topcoat over top of the Scratch Sealer.

35 Here we are using an airbrush to spray Scratch Sealer on the left shoe. Scratch Sealer is a water-based topcoat agent, so it doesn't require a special dilution solution and is quite easy to use. That being said, dry times are longer when diluted with water, so remember to allow more time for your sneakers to dry than you would if applying undiluted Scratch Sealer with a brush.

36 The right shoe is given the topcoat treatment next. Once the Scratch Sealer dries, remove the masking tape and we're done. It's exciting to see the end result of this NIKE x Travis Scott Air Max 270 model customization, where we employed stencil vinyl instead of the NIKE-recommended sticker paper.

>>

CUSTOMIZATION SKILL

Removing Masking Tape
Checking Differences in the Finished Product

This is the final step of the stencil customization process, where we overcome the unexpected problem of the stencil not fitting the sneaker using the officially recommended method. Make sure the topcoat is dry, and remove the masking tape.

Is there any difference in the finished product between the left shoe, which the customizer worked on according to the official instructions, and the right shoe, which he solved using his own ideas?

37 After touching the painted surface with your fingers and making sure the topcoat is dry, remove the tape. That moment when the orange-tinted Swoosh appears is very impressive. At first glance, the Swoosh seems to be painted on both the left and right sides without any problems, but I wonder if the difference is apparent in the details.

38 Close-up of the left shoe. This one used paper stickers and followed the recommended process. The customizer adjusted the direction of the airbrush to keep the paint from blowing into the gaps between the stencils. That is why the edges are a bit blurry. All in all, this is an acceptable result that creates a stencil-like look.

39 A close-up of the right shoe. Here a stencil vinyl sheet was used. It is hard to tell the difference from a distance, but up close you can clearly see the sharp, defined edges. It is worth mentioning the fact that this finish was achieved without paying close attention to the direction of the airbrush flow.

40 In conclusion, when stenciling the Air Max 270, it is recommended that you use vinyl stencils. They conform to the shoe better and are much easier to work with. In the end, I believe that ideas that can improve efficiency and make customization more fun should be shared.

>>

Complete

CUSTOMIZATION SKILL

The Swoosh Is Complete
You Can Overcome Any Customization Obstacles You Face

This stenciled-on Swoosh project started because "it is officially recommended by the manufacturer." As we proceeded with the actual work, it became clear that it would not be an easy customization job that everyone could enjoy. There would certainly be some hurdles for beginners. That being said, those who don't want to make the effort to overcome such hurdles will probably not want to customize their own sneakers in the first place. Those who want to try it after seeing the examples presented here will surely be able to overcome such obstacles. "Creator's One: Monozukuri Working Space," which worked on this customization, is a place that provides the necessary facilities and know-how to overcome customization challenges. Before worrying about which problems you might face, I would advise you to visit workshops staffed by those with a wealth of experience in customization.

The Orange on Your Feet Swooshes Along, Making Sneaker Fans Turn Around

STENCIL PAINTING
NIKE ×TRAVIS SCOTT AIR MAX 270 "CACTUS TRAILS"

CASE STUDY
#05
CARTOON PAINT

CASE STUDY
#05
CARTOON PAINT CUSTOMIZATION

CASE STUDY #05

CARTOON PAINT CUSTOMIZATION >>
NIKE AIR FORCE 1 LOW

It's Like Something out of a Comic Book: Playful and Artistic Customization

Sneakers depicted in cartoons and illustrations tend to have a unique style. "Cartoon painting" is a way to re-create this style on real sneakers. Although this is a relatively minor genre in Japan, it definitely pops up at sneaker-related events. Here, we interviewed Shu Asaoka—a popular YouTuber who provides all kinds of information on sneakers—and had him introduce the process of applying cartoon paint to standard Air Force 1 models.

In Cooperation with YouTube Channel "Shu Asaoka & The Jack Band"

Start

CUSTOMIZATION
SKILL

Masking Off the Midsole
Apply Masking Tape All the Way around the Midsole

This time, we selected the all-white NIKE Air Force 1 Low as the base for our customization. Their white leather parts are probably the most popular product in the world for customization because of their amazing color when painted. The only problem is that they are relatively hard to find, since they are very popular even in their precustomized state. The eyelets will also be painted this time, so be sure to remove the shoelaces beforehand.

01 The Air Force 1, originally released in 1982, is an all-white, coordinated low-cut model that has become one of the most popular sneaker models in the world. It is rapidly becoming the most popular base for custom-painted sneakers as well. Here, we will create a tasteful custom sneaker by applying cartoon paint to this classic sneaker.

02 Masking tape is applied to the midsole in order to be sure that the cartoon paint is applied only to the upper this time. If you are not familiar with painting sneakers, it is a good idea to prep the tongue by covering it with a plastic bag—secured with masking tape—so that the paint doesn't stick to it.

03 After masking tape has been applied to the midsole. Be sure to apply masking tape along the border between the upper and the midsole. Note that when painting with an airbrush or sprayer, it is best to apply masking tape to the entire sole, since paint tends to splatter.

04 After finishing the masking treatment, the surface to be painted is prepared. Many sneakers on the market have oil on their surface. If you paint them as they are, it probably won't go well. In order to avoid problems with paint not sticking, it is important to wipe off the oil / factory finish, using a commercially available lacquer thinner or acetone.

Pretreatment of Target Surfaces
Clean Target Surfaces as If Peeling Off Thin Skin

It's important to note that the pretreatment process for painted surfaces differs depending on the material. For smooth leather (grain side of leather), lacquer or acetone can be used, but for patent leather, which is quite sensitive to solvents, it is safer to just clean the surface with a neutral detergent. For suede, nubuck, and other materials that are susceptible to liquid penetration, it is best to just use a shoe brush to clean the surface.

05 Use lacquer thinner to prep the surface. Wipe upward toward the tongue of the shoe. Some sneakers have both oil and a factory coating on their surface. In either case, it is best to wipe the surface as if you were peeling off a thin layer of skin.

06 In this example, lacquer has been applied to a dollar store cotton pad. If you use a melamine sponge, also available at the dollar store, you can attenuate the risk of fibers sticking to the surface of the sneakers. On the other hand, you may apply too much force when using a sponge. In the end, it is best to choose the method that you are most comfortable with.

07 Here, the entire upper has been wiped down with lacquer thinner. It is hard to tell from the image, but when you check the actual surface, you can see that the gloss is almost gone. Although lacquer and acetone volatilize quickly, it is definitely necessary to allow enough time for the surface to dry thoroughly. While we are waiting, we can prep the other shoe.

08 Angelus Paint's "Gift Box Blue" will be used as our main color this time. This vivid color is reminiscent of a Luxury brand gift box. It goes well with a white base. This is a standard Angelus Paint color that many customizers use on their sneakers.

>>

CUSTOMIZATION SKILL

Painting Toe Cap and Heel
First Step in Establishing a Customizer's Sense of Style

Once pre-treatment is complete, apply the main color that will determine the overall impression of the shoe. When custom-painting sneakers, it is necessary to balance the parts to be painted with those that will remain in the base color. Just remember to keep the finished product in mind. The process of selecting the parts to be painted is a step that tests the customizer's sense of style.

09 The main parts to be painted in Gift Box Blue are the toe cap, eyestays, heel, and Swoosh. These are the color panels that represent the Air Force 1, and instead of trying to be different, we are just going to add our own individuality to the iconic "Air Force 1 style."

10 Here, the toe cap is painted Gift Box Blue. Although it depends on the color used, Angelus Paint generally has excellent concealment property (ability to hide the base color). It is also rated as a paint that doesn't produce uneven strokes. When applied on a white base, which improves color, it is nice to know that it is possible to get reasonable concealment from a single coat.

11 Next, we'll paint the eyestays and heel. To paint these parts without masking, it is relatively easy to just brush from the inside toward the cross section of the parts, taking advantage of differences in height as a border. However, it takes experience to acquire this skill, so if you are not used to it, mask off the parts not to be painted.

12 After painting each part, dry with a heat gun or hairdryer. The reason we do this is that the longer it takes to dry, the more likely dust will stick to everything. If you don't notice dust sticking to the surface and subsequently allow the paint to dry, it will leave marks. Drying frequently is the only way to avoid unnecessary work.

>>

Apply Two Coats to Swoosh
Apply Second Coat to Remove Uneven Brushstrokes

Next, we move on to paint the Swoosh. For those of you who already know a bit about DIY customization, you probably also know that it is better to apply multiple thin layers of paint, allowing each layer to dry between coats, than to apply one thick coat. This will not only prevent paint dripping or streaking but also make the surface finish much more beautiful. This is actually a basic principle of painting, not just for sneakers.

13 Paint the Swoosh with Gift Box Blue, being careful not to let the paint hit any nontarget areas. It is all right to paint with brushes purchased at dollar stores, but be aware that the tips on many inexpensive brushes can split open during painting. This could make the paint run. Brushes are the one tool that can easily show the difference between high and low quality.

14 After completing the Swoosh, the surface should be dried again, using a heat gun or hairdryer. This is a rather simple routine when compared to the process of determining the desired paint scheme, but it is a fact that more-advanced customizers repeat the drying process rather frequently. Also, it isn't hard to imagine just how much of an impact the drying has on the overall finish.

15 After the Swoosh, paint the logo embroidered on the heel. This is a delicate job that requires the use of a very fine brush, but if you allow the paint to soak into the embroidery—rather than forcing it in—the result will be surprisingly beautiful. If any paint protrudes from the target area, quickly wipe it off with a cotton swab.

16 After confirming that the painted logo is dry, apply second coats to all of the painted parts to remove any uneven brushstrokes on the surface. Angelus Paint should be used sparingly, and the work should be done quickly so that the paint layers are thin. Always be careful not to let paint flow over the edge of the target part. If you brush perpendicular to the unevenness, you will get an even more beautiful finish.

>>

How to Proceed with Cartoon Painting

Add White Highlights, Referring to a Comic If Available

Once the main color is complete, it is time to apply the "cartoon" paint. In this example, it isn't monotone. Rather, it is a full-color comic book cartoon paint. The idea of the customization was to create a "blur" effect caused by reflections and mimic a cartoon character's movements in the design of the Air Force 1. If you stay bold and don't fear failure, this painting process will produce the correct image.

17 The main color scheme has been added to the Air Force 1. This is the last time we will be using the Gift Box Blue paint, so don't forget to clean your brushes and close the lids on any open containers. These custom sneakers look cool enough as they are, but let's move on to produce that cartoon feel we originally planned to create.

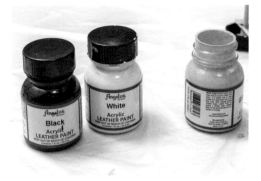

18 The key to cartoon painting is to use monotone colors, such as white and black, to create "comic-like" details. Here again, we will use Angelus Paint in white and black. As long as the previous Angelus Paint has dried, there is no need to worry about color mixing when applying different colors of paint.

19 Draw short white lines along the stitching of the parts painted in Gift Box Blue. In many full-color comics, highlights are drawn to emphasize details by creating the image of reflected light. Use this technique to draw cartoon-painting lines.

20 Add a series of short white lines to each part to make the edges pop. Use short brushstrokes at the edges in order to create a sense of agileness. If you go overboard here, you can easily recover the original feel by simply repainting with Gift Box Blue. So, don't be afraid to make mistakes and paint boldly.

>>

Add Highlights to the Upper
Let's Add White Lines to Produce "Reflections"

In many cases, white and black will be used for the highlight color. It is important to note the difference in characteristics between white and black. When painting highlights on a light base, as in this case, white is relatively unnoticeable, but when painting on a dark base such as navy, white becomes very noticeable. Adjusting the balance between white and black is the key to success.

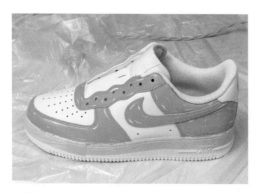

21 Check out the highlights, painted in white, on the outside of the upper. The toe cap, Swoosh, and other parts of the upper are evenly highlighted. But the overall tone of the paint is bright, and you can see that the cartoon-painted look is not that pronounced.

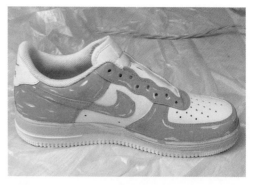

22 Here we see the white highlights on the instep. Note that highlights are also drawn on the collar, heel counter, and eyestays. If it is hard to see where the highlights should be, you can take a picture of the sneaker with your smartphone under a bright light and place the highlights wherever you notice reflections.

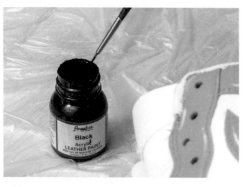

23 After checking the balance of the white highlights, paint the shadows black. Angelus black is used here. The sheen of your dried paint will vary depending on the type of paint used. But, given that the surface sheen can be adjusted during the topcoat process, there is no need to worry about it at this stage.

24 Use a thin brush to add shadows to the upper. With the color scheme selected for this project, the black is very noticeable and will greatly affect the finished product. Even though it isn't very difficult to fix mistakes, it is still recommended to proceed with more caution than when adding white highlights.

>>

CUSTOMIZATION SKILL

Adding Shadows with Black Paint

At This Stage, Less Is More

After the white highlights are drawn, add black shadows. For the sake of convenience, we use the word "shadow," but it doesn't just mean to adding lines to express shadows. You also need to create details with rough lines, as seen in action comics.

That being said, black lines are very noticeable, so be careful not to overdo it. If you go overboard, the finished product will just look like a "dirty sneaker" instead of a nice cartoon painting.

25 If you are using colored sneakers as a base, black accents on the borders of all the parts would appear too harsh. First, let's imagine how the shadows might appear, and draw them in.

26 Black is also used around the eyelets to emphasize detail. If you surround the eyelets with a solid line, it will be too conspicuous. However, if you draw rough broken lines around the details—like you would in a comic book draft—you will produce a softer, less conspicuous feel. You can also change the lines, depending on their position, for different looks.

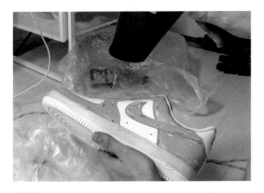

27 After painting the shadows, don't forget to dry them as usual. If you are trying this process for the first time, it is probably best to paint a little bit at a time on each side and adjust the balance as you go along. If you get stuck, it is not a bad idea to look at your favorite manga or comic books for inspiration.

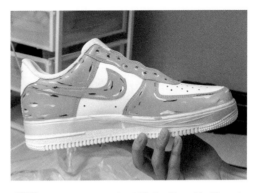

28 Here are the parts, painted Gift Box Blue, with white and black lines added for emphasis. At this stage, it may look a bit quiet for a cartoon paint job, but since we will be adding more shadows on the white parts later, it is only right that they appear a little underdone right now.

>>

Highlighting the Ventilation Holes

Painting the Small Ventilation Holes on Each Part

One of the most effective techniques for emphasizing the cartoonlike feel of a shoe is to color the ventilation holes. Ventilation holes are usually represented as "black dots" in comics and illustrations, whereas in real sneakers they are actual "holes." In other words, if the ventilation holes appear black, the cartoonlike impression of the shoe increases dramatically.

29 An effective technique for making ventilation holes look like "black dots" is to paint their edges black. In the case of the Air Force 1, the ventilation hole edges are only a few millimeters in diameter, and by simply painting the edges black, the look of the "black dots" can be emphasized to an unexpected degree.

30 Here the edge of the-left shoe ventilation holes has been painted black. Even though the size of the hole has not been altered, the detail has been emphasized, giving the shoe a more cartoonish look. It should be noted that painting the edges of the eyelets themselves is not recommended because of the risk of color fading due to friction.

31 Similar to above, the ventilation hole edges on the midsection are painted black. Needless to say, painting the edges black will be useless if the base color is dark. In that case, paint the edges white or silver, and check the overall balance before proceeding.

32 After the edges have been colored, add black lines to emphasize the ventilation holes and Swoosh. Lines around the ventilation holes will give a particularly strong impression that is typical of a cartoon paint job. So, it is a good idea to incorporate this into the finishing touches of the toe area.

>>

CUSTOMIZATION SKILL

Fine-Tuning Cartoon Paint
Sometimes It's Necessary to Add Base Color to Conceal Cartoon Painting

Adding cartoonlike touch-ups is the final step. This is where the details and the final balance are adjusted. Unlike standard custom painting, where each part is painted and it is easy to imagine what the finished product will look like, with cartoon painting, you really don't know until you try. Adjusting the final balance is an important process that greatly affects the apparent degree of completion.

33 Draw shadows along the heel logo to highlight it. Instead of just encircling the logo in black, leave some white space between the Gift Box Blue and black. The white areas will accentuate both the blue and the black.

34 The Air Force 1 also has a leather tongue, so shadows will be added here as well. If the tongue material is mesh, Angelus Paint should not be applied directly. Rather, the paint on the tongue should have Angelus 2-Soft added (sold separately). If the procedure isn't followed, the painted surface will crack easily.

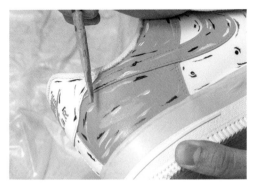

35 After adding shadows to the heel and tongue, check the overall balance once again. If you find any areas that really stand out in a bad way at this point, it's best to apply Gift Box Blue again. Here, the adjustment needed is to fill in some of the shadows to make the Gift Box Blue on the heel parts stand out more.

36 Once the overall balance is achieved, thread the shoelaces. Even though the tongue shadows won't be that noticeable, it is natural to paint the parts that are not visible, in order to increase the level of perfection. Different-colored shoelaces can be used at this point, but we chose white for balance.

>>

CUSTOMIZATION SKILL

Topcoat and Paint the Shoelaces
Use a Topcoat to Increase the Overall Shine

To finish off the paint job, add shadows to the shoelaces and apply topcoat to the entire upper. Up to this point in the process, there has been a difference in the amount of gloss on the painted and unpainted parts. Topcoating not only makes the paint less likely to fade but also helps balance the overall luster. Even if the topcoat treatment doesn't make a difference in the coloring, it is a process that should not be omitted, since it offers many advantages.

37 To emphasize shoelace detail, shadows are added. Once you actually put these shoes on, you may want to add shadows to areas where the shoelaces are now exposed. It is a quick and easy "one step" fix, but the effect is huge and will make your feet look absolutely unique.

38 Remove masking tape from midsole area. The contrast between the uniquely tailored upper and the simple sole unit is quite beautiful. For a more casual look, you can paint the "AIR" logo on the midsole in Gift Box Blue and add a shadow around it

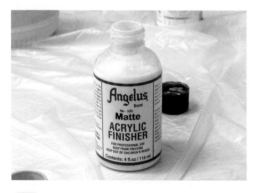

39 Always apply a topcoat to finish your custom paint job. The topcoat used here is Angelus Paint's Matte Acrylic Finisher. It's the "Matte" type, so it will dry to a wonderful matte finish. This topcoat gives the leather a natural sheen, as opposed to a nubuck look.

40 Use a brush to apply Matte Acrylic Finisher to the entire upper. Topcoating not just the painted areas, but also the unpainted areas, adjusts the overall luster of the shoe. There are different types of Acrylic Finisher available from Angelus Paint. Feel free to choose the one that best suits your needs.

NIKE AIR FORCE 1 LOW

Complete

CUSTOMIZATION SKILL

Completed Cartoon-Painted Custom Sneakers
Artistic Custom Sneakers that Say "Manga Culture"

Many of the custom sneakers enjoyed in Japan tend to be iconic models that everyone admires, or premier models that are hard to find. However, in the rest of the world, artistic customization that expresses the individuality of the customizer—rather than copying an existing design—has become the norm. Still, it would not be an exaggeration to say that cartoon-painted sneakers, which incorporate Japanese manga culture into their design, are one of the most popular sneaker customizations in the world.

"Shu Asaoka & The Jack Band" is a YouTube channel run by Shu Asaoka, who worked on this customization. In addition to information about sneakers, he also introduces customization examples such as sneaker rusting. If you're interested in videos that will make your daily sneaker life more enjoyable, don't forget to subscribe to the channel!

CUSTOMIZER INFORMATION

YouTuber: Shu Asaoka

Shu Asaoka & The Jack Band
https://www.youtube.com/channel/
UCu3VsuMU3qA9fAumWtpUqsw/

Straight Out of a Comic Book:

An Irresistible "Subculture" Feel

CARTOON PAINT CUSTOMIZATION
NIKE AIR FORCE 1 LOW

CASE STUDY
#06
STREET
ART
PAINTING

CASE STUDY
#06
STREET ART PAINTING

STREET ART PAINTING >>
NIKE AIR JORDAN 1 RETRO HIGH OG "METALLIC RED"

Airbrushing Sneakers:
Creating Custom Sneakers with Gradated Coloring

The most common method of custom-painting sneakers is to brush on paint. This is due to the fact that brush painting is easy and fun, and also because it is easy to achieve a beautiful finish with sneaker paints. However, in the DIY world, airbrush painting is also becoming popular. In this section, we will head to rental space equipped with model paint booths, and introduce street art–style custom painting using airbrushed gradations.

In Cooperation with: Creator's One: Monozukuri Working Space

Start

CUSTOMIZATION SKILL 1

Masking Off Sneakers

Careful Masking Greatly Affects the Appearance of the Finished Product

The NIKE Air Jordan 1 Retro High OG in "Metallic Red" forms the base of this customization. These sneakers are rapidly gaining popularity as a base for custom sneakers because of the large white areas. Let's take this old-school classic sneaker, with its white base and red color, and airbrush it into a customized sneaker with a street feel.

01 These Air Jordan 1s are reproduced in the traditional color, so genuine sneaker fans might get offended and say, "What the heck are you doing painting Air Jordan 1s!?" But the truth is that this pair was purchased at an outlet store before the recent boom and cost less than ⅓ of aftermarket price. So, let's not think of it as a waste of money, and just go ahead and paint them to look good.

02 We are going to be airbrushing only the upper, so let's mask off the entire midsole first. Use wider masking tape for the midsole. Many old-school basketball shoes, like the Air Jordan 1, have straight lines at the sole joint. That's why the midsole is treated with wide masking tape.

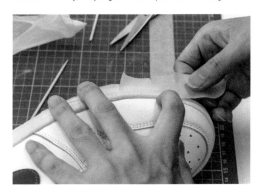

03 For subtly curved areas, such as the tip, another technique is to cut slits into the masking tape to make it easier to follow the curve. Some hobby stores sell masking tape made of a plastic material that can handle curves, but it tends to be too narrow to be suitable for masking large surfaces.

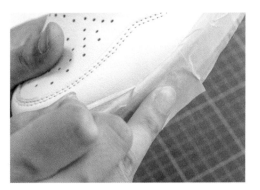

04 Tape that protrudes from the upper edge of the midsole can be manipulated with the tip of a toothpick. Masking tape used for customizing sneakers can be purchased at a dollar store, but such tape will often have poor adhesion. It is best to get your tape from a home improvement store whenever possible.

CUSTOMIZATION SKILL

Sneaker Masking
Using Masking Tape and Plastic Bags Increases Efficiency

Masking your sneakers with tape isn't the only way to get the job done. Since different parts of the sneakers have different shapes, materials, and sizes, it is important to use materials that are familiar to you, in order to improve efficiency. In this case, ordinary masking tape and a plastic bag from the dollar store are used to mask the entire shoe.

05 Use a precision knife to cut open the plastic bag and attach it to the bottom of the shoes. Apply masking tape to the edge of the plastic bag first. Then, apply in a similar manner to the masking tape around the border of the midsole. Once you get used to it, it is much easier than putting masking tape all over the bottom of the entire shoe. You can cover all the gaps easily.

06 The soft shoe tongue is first covered with a plastic bag and then taped at the base of the tongue. If you're a customizer, you've probably already experienced trying to cover all of these parts with masking tape and losing your mind.

07 After applying masking tape on the Swoosh and collar, use a precision knife to cut out the Swoosh. If the blade isn't sharp enough, it is easy to make mistakes by using excessive force. Masking tape isn't applied to the embossed wings on the ankles, because they are really complicated and similar red paint will be applied.

08 Air Jordan 1 all masked up. If you want to mask off the Jordan Wings logo, you can either do the entire logo and adjust it later or apply paintable, removable rubber and just emboss that and remove it later. However, perfect masking of these types of logo is extremely difficult, so a certain amount of compromise may be necessary.

Surface Preparation
Prepare by Applying Acetone and Scratch Sealer

CUSTOMIZATION SKILL

Even if you use paint designed for sneakers, there is a high risk of the paint peeling off when worn. Regardless of whether you are using a brush or an airbrush, it is always a good idea to prepare a good base for your custom sneakers. In this section,

we'll be using acetone and Raleigh Restoration's Scratch Resistant Sealer, a topcoat that is known for its strength. Let's get started.

09 Acetone reliably removes oil from painted surfaces and is best used by transferring it, via an eyedropper, to a dollar store plastic bottle with a pump. However, storing acetone for long periods of time in standard dollar store bottles may be unsafe. So, it's best to dispose of the leftover acetone in the bottle or return it to the original can when finished.

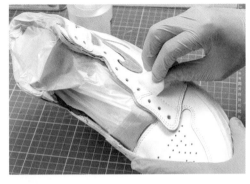

10 Use a melamine sponge and acetone to quickly remove surface oil. Note that the patent leather (varnish) used for the Swoosh will turn cloudy when acetone is applied. If the surface to be glued is more delicate than the Swoosh in our example, use a pretreater that won't damage the material, such as Angelus Deglazer.

11 At the suggestion of the rental space staff, we decided to use Raleigh Restoration's Scratch Resistant Sealer as a primer to improve paint adhesion. It is a topcoat material originally prepared for finishing, but since it can be painted over after it dries, they decided to use it as a primer as well.

12 Apply Scratch Resistant Sealer to the entire target surface. It is cloudy white in the bottle, but when it dries it becomes colorless and transparent. So, you can use it even if you are using a colored base. When it dries, it becomes matte, so it is easy to check if you forgot to apply it or not by checking just the level of surface gloss.

>>

Understanding Properties of Sneaker Paint
Diluting Paint Is a Cardinal Rule

Once the surface has been prepped, we proceed to the airbrushing process. When painting with a brush, Angelus Paint is generally not diluted, but when using an airbrush, it is necessary to dilute to one-half or one-third its original strength, using a suitable thinner. This applies not only to Angelus Paint but to other paints as well. So, be sure to prepare a set of paints and thinner when airbrushing.

13 In the example shown here, we will be applying "Varsity," inspired by the red in NIKE sneakers. First of all, shake the bottle to mix up the contents. Water-based acrylic paints harden when exposed to air, so opening the lid and stirring with a brush will only shorten the life of the paint.

14 Transfer the proper amount of paint to a paper cup. If you use a bamboo skewer or toothpick, the rim of the bottle won't get so dirty. The rental space staff, who are skilled in handling paint, should be just full of ideas for you. There is also a good reason why paper cups are used as containers when transferring paint. We will get into that later.

15 Add Angelus 2-Thin to the paint to adjust the concentration. For water-based acrylic paints, it is common to add together equal parts thinner and paint. Angelus 2-Thin is a must-have for Angelus Paint users, since it can be used to adjust paint that has become too thick after long-term storage.

16 Use a bamboo skewer or toothpick to stir the paint. This time we used Angelus Paint alone, but when using mixed colors, a slight difference in the distribution of the paint will cause the color to change. So, it's best to prepare a little extra. If you can't get all of the paint in your airbrush, wrap the excess in a paper cup or store it in a separate jar.

>>

Airbrush Preparation
Compatible Airbrushes and Paint

CUSTOMIZATION SKILL

Once your paint is ready, it is time to start airbrushing. "Creator's One: Monozukuri Working Space," the rental space we visited this time, is equipped with rental airbrushes and painting booths. However, I brought a portable mini airbrush with compact compressor (which can be purchased on Amazon for around 80 dollars) to enjoy painting more easily. Careful though: there is a pitfall lurking in this airbrush that a novice would find difficult to notice.

17 Here, we are pouring adjusted Angelus Paint into the airbrush paint cup brought in by the editorial team. When using a paper cup to adjust the paint density or color, it is easy to pinch the edge and pour directly into the airbrush's small paint cup. This idea came from the staff, who have a wealth of experience handling airbrushes.

18 After test-spraying on a piece of white paper, the paint was forming lumps. This phenomenon tends to occur when the paint is too thick, but in this case, that didn't seem to be the problem. Perhaps the compressor is too weak to reach the right pressure for Angelus Paint.

19 In order to verify the cause of the roughness, we compared the airbrush with one from the rental space. The store airbrush uses a stationary compressor, which ensures sufficient pressure. When the same paint was sprayed with this airbrush, the result was obvious: a beautifully gradated pattern.

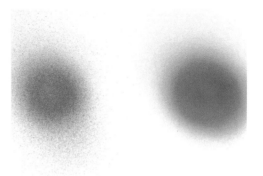

20 The test pattern on the left is from the mini airbrush, while the right is from an air brush provided by the rental space. Water-based acrylic paints such as Angelus Paint are heavier than others and require relatively high pressure. Since the pressure required varies from paint to paint, it is impossible to give a clear indication of which airbrush you should purchase, but it is certainly wise to consult someone familiar with airbrushes before purchasing one.

>>

Custom Airbrush Painting
Techniques for Creating a Street Art Look

CUSTOMIZATION SKILL

This project makes use of characteristic airbrush techniques to paint the entire upper in a street art style. The finished image is reminiscent of the famous NIKE "Dunk Haze," released in 2003. That particular sneaker re-created a graffiti-like atmosphere of street art. Let's change the image of the original Air Jordan 1 with its old-school feel into a special custom sneaker that exudes underground street style.

21 The "Dunk Haze," used as a reference for the finished image here, emphasized details by applying a single-colored gradation to the upper. In order to re-create this unique detail in our custom paint job, Angelus Paint was first used to draw a line along the border of the parts.

22 The boundary lines of the parts that make up the upper are painted. Continue airbrushing with the image of expanding those boundary lines. Angelus Paint's "Varsity" color—which is slightly more magenta than the standard water-based acrylic red—is used here because it can reproduce colors similar to the Jordan Wings logo on the ankle without mixing multiple paints.

23 Apply paint to the areas inside the red painted lines. In order to create a street art look, the areas close to the painted lines are painted darker, while the areas farther away grow lighter and lighter. Don't forget to keep in mind that when the masking tape is removed, the dark-red parts of the Swoosh and collar will be exposed.

24 After gradating the entire shoe, check the balance. If you feel that the color is not dark enough, or if there are areas that you want to emphasize in terms of design, add additional paint. On the other hand, if you feel that the color is too dark, don't panic; just use acetone to remove the dark areas and then repaint the shoe after doing the base treatment again.

>>

CUSTOMIZATION SKILL 7

Custom Airbrush Painting
Introducing a Secret Weapon to Reduce Drying Time

Next, the remaining shoe is painted. This is a custom model with a distinctive appearance, so the painted surface should be dried as quickly as possible, and then the balance between the left and right shoes can be checked. Though not a method recommended by appliance

manufacturers, I should mention that it Is not uncommon in the hobby industry to use countertop dish dryers for drying shoes. The workshop rental space where we worked on this project had one on hand.

25 Put the sneakers in the dish dryer to reduce drying time. Although a covered dryer reduces the risk of dust sticking to the painted surface, putting sneakers in your own dryer will inevitably elicit a fierce reaction from the family. If you want to make use of this "secret weapon," you'd have to buy a dryer dedicated for your paintwork.

26 Using the dried shoe as a guide, we can now apply the gradation paint to the other shoe. The first step is to draw a line along the border of the parts and then apply the gradation inside the line. Unlike general painting, where you have to be careful not to leave any unpainted areas, gradation painting requires a sense of how to make the most of the base color.

27 Here are both gradated shoes. Let's put both shoes side by side to adjust the details. Although the white parts are a bit obvious in the image, there are dark-red parts hidden under the masking tape, and the shoes will have red laces when worn. So, at this point it seems best to just leave the paint as is. It is tempting to add a bit more color, but sometimes it's best to just stop.

28 After painting is complete, the entire upper is sprayed with a topcoat. Since the topcoat will also be airbrushed this time, the handpiece must be cleaned carefully. Water-based acrylic paints can be cleaned with water, but a special cleaner will improve efficiency. In this case, brush cleaner sold by Angelus was used.

CUSTOMIZATION SKILL

Topcoat Treatment and Masking-Tape Removal
Coat Surface with Same Scratch-Resistant Sealer Used for the Primer

The final phase of this street art-style customization. A topcoat is applied to protect the painted surface. There are a variety of topcoats available for sneakers, but we will use the same Scratch Resistant Sealer that we used for the primer. This topcoat has a good reputation for increasing the strength of the painted surface and is used by many customizers. It is water-based and easy to use and is recommended for custom paint beginners.

29 Applying undiluted Scratch Resistant Sealer with a brush is fine, but in this case, since it will be sprayed on, it should be diluted about 1.5:1 with tap water. In general, water-based topcoats take longer to dry when diluted with water, but don't worry: if you apply heat with a heat gun or a dish dryer, it won't take so long that your work will be delayed.

30 Spray the entire painted surface with Scratch Resistant Sealer. This is a colorless and transparent topcoat, so it might be difficult to see where it has been applied. Don't worry though; it is safe to apply two or three coats as long as it is not too thick. If you are not sure if you already applied one coat, don't hesitate to spray one on anyway.

31 Once the topcoat is completely dry, remove the masking tape and the plastic bag. The Jordan Wings logos on the ankles are not masked, but the original details are clearly visible because the same color of paint was just thinly sprayed. This finish is quite difficult to achieve with brush painting.

32 After removing tape from the shoes, we're done! In this case, we used Scratch Resistant Sealer for the topcoat, so the painted surface is matte. If you want a semiglossy or glossy surface, you can apply Angelus brand Acrylic Finisher over the Scratch Resistant Sealer.

>>

Complete

CUSTOMIZATION
SKILL

Complete Custom Sneakers in the Street Art Style
One-of-a-Kind Custom Sneakers

It is no exaggeration to say that a pair of custom sneakers with a gradated paint job that varies slightly depending on the taste and skill of the creator is truly a one-of-a-kind custom sneaker. This time, instead of customization builders who have a strong preconceived notion about sneakers, we dared to ask a workshop rental space to help out. As a result, not only did we get some unique custom sneakers, we also got a lot of ideas to make the painting process easler. "Creator's One: Monozukuri Working Space" offers a wide variety of opportunities for "monozukuri" (making things), in many mediums. It is a professional store that provides the know-how of its staff with a wealth of experience. The store also offers workshops and consultation programs for those who are looking to improve their customization skills. In other words, it is well worth the visit.

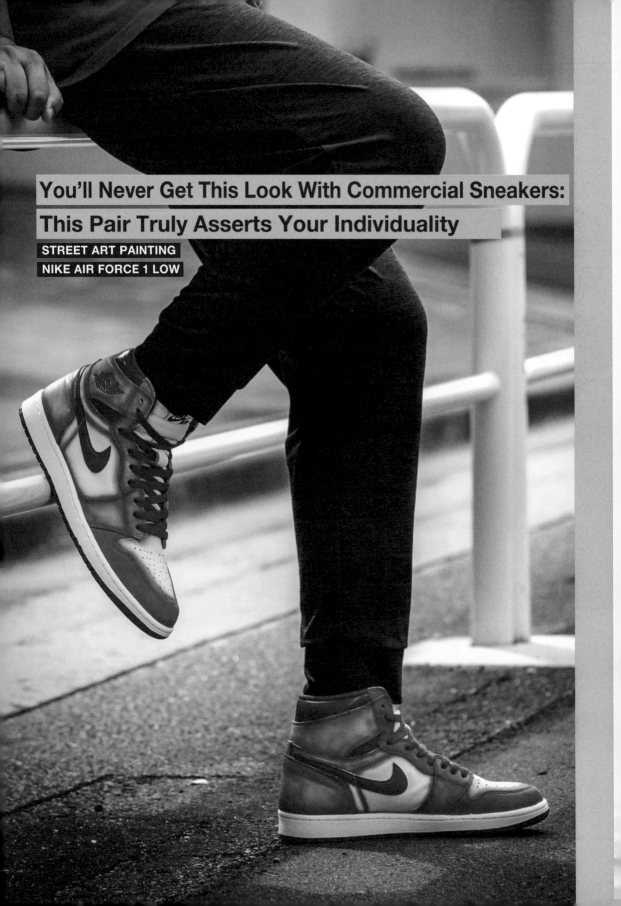

You'll Never Get This Look With Commercial Sneakers: This Pair Truly Asserts Your Individuality

STREET ART PAINTING
NIKE AIR FORCE 1 LOW

CASE STUDY
#07
STYLE CHANGE

#07
STYLE CHANGE CUSTOMIZATION

CASE STUDY #07

STYLE CHANGE CUSTOMIZATION >>
NIKE AIR JORDAN 1 HIGH OG "BLOODLINE"

Altering Styles—"Bloodline" to "Chicago": Turning Easy-to-Obtain Air Jordan 1s into Everyone's Dream Sneakers

The Air Jordan 1, originally introduced in 1982, is one of the most popular sneakers in the world, especially the "Chicago" color. Color reprints are even so popular that they sell out instantly. If you're lucky enough to obtain a pair, you might be hesitant to wear them because of their high resale value. If that's the case, you can always custom-paint your own Air Jordans in the "Chicago" color. Let's take a look at the process of custom painting a pair of "Bloodline" shoes in the "Chicago" color. This has become a superhot topic on Instagram.

In Cooperation with: JUNKYARD Koenji

Major Skills Acquired
■ Pretreatment of Target Surfaces .... P. 067
■ Painting Base Color .... P. 068
■ Finishing Color Mixing .... P. 070
■ Finishing Up the Jordan Wings Logo .... P. 074

Start

CUSTOMIZATION SKILL 1

Pretreatment of Target Surfaces

Professionals Use a Shoe Brush to Complete Surface Prep

Acetone is used to remove the coating on commercial sneakers. While the coating has the advantage of repelling dirt and other contaminants, it also makes it difficult for paint to penetrate the surface. Acetone and other solvents can damage the material, so don't overdo it. Still, it is a process that professionals and amateurs alike cannot avoid when custom-painting sneakers.

01 Clean the surface with acetone on a cotton pad. In the examples shown here, most of the work involves changing the black parts to red. When changing black to other colors, it is necessary to paint with a certain thickness. Don't forget to do a thorough pretreatment to help the paint stick.

02 When using acetone, it is best to transfer it from the can to another container with an eyedropper—or something similar—before proceeding. The type shown in the photo is excellent, since just small amount of acetone comes out when you push the plate on top. Professional stores generally find them very useful.

03 Once the black-dyed leather parts are wiped with acetone, the black paint will come off on the degreased cotton. You can literally feel how strong the acetone is. When pretreating white leather parts, it is difficult to see the paint peeling off, and you run the risk of using more acetone than necessary.

04 Once the acetone has dried, clean with a towel or shoe brush. If black paint flakes are left on the leather or stitching, they may stand out like dust when bright paint is applied. This is the professional way to minimize such a risk.

CUSTOMIZATION SKILL 2

Painting Base Color
Painting Process That Supports Proper Coloration

The base color is added after the pretreatment. The Angelus Paint used here reproduces the colors used in sneakers, but if the base color is too strong, it will show through. This makes it difficult to achieve the true color. That being said, it is necessary to apply a base color before applying the main color in order to obtain the correct tone. Here, "LILAC" from Angelus Paint was used.

05 White is often used as a base color for custom paint. However, the customizer who worked on this project uses Angelus Paint's Lilac. This is an original recipe devised by our customizers, and it is based on tons of experience. They said that the Lilac base color is essential to reproduce the typical Air Jordan 1 red.

06 Apply base color around the Jordan Wings logo using a very fine brush. Perhaps a script liner brush that can be purchased at a hobby store or an art supply store. This is the most difficult part of the custom-painting process for the Air Jordan 1.

07 When applying the base color around the Jordan Wings logo, it's best to use a heat gun to dry the painted surface in small increments. It's always possible that you will accidently touch a still-wet area by mistake while concentrating on painting. If you keep the painted surface dry, even if you touch the painted area by mistake, you will be able to avoid the worst-case scenarios and the need to start over.

08 After applying Lilac around the Jordan Wings logo, let's apply the base color to the other parts. Since we are going to change all the parts from black to red, except for the Swoosh and the rubber on the collar, we will have to repaint quite a few areas. Use a wider brush than the one you used in the previous step, and you can work at a faster pace.

>>

Finish Painting Base Color

If the Base Color Isn't Done Carefully, It Won't Be Pro-Level Quality

CUSTOMIZATION SKILL

All the parts that go from black to red will be coated with Angelus Paint's Lilac. Even though this is a base coat, if there is any unevenness, there is a high risk that it will adversely affect the finished look. Let's not cut corners just because it is a base

coat. Let it dry and then apply a second coat to make sure the paint is evenly distributed. After the base is complete, apply Scratch Sealer to increase strength.

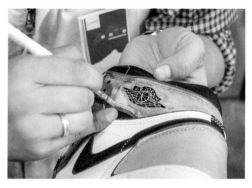

09 Apply base color to target areas. Even though Angelus Paint has excellent concealment properties, a single coat on black will always result in an uneven finish. Even if it is just a base coat, apply two separate coats just as you would for a real custom paint job. This will create a solid base.

10 The area around the Jordan Wings logo, detailed earlier, is now painted. If there is a small amount of paint protruding, it can easily be fixed by using black paint in the finishing process. First of all, it is important to paint the Lilac on every detail to produce that special Air Jordan 1 red.

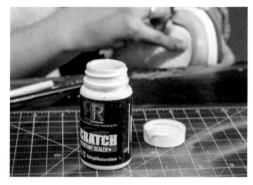

11 After the base coat has been applied, apply Scratch Sealer to the entire area. Scratch Sealer not only increases strength, it also improves paint adhesion. Interestingly, many customizers we interviewed for this book used it as both a primer and a topcoat.

12 After applying the Scratch Sealer, it must be allowed to dry thoroughly. Even though we have done only the base coat, you can see that even in this state, the quality is good enough to be a customization in and of itself. In other words, if the base isn't finished to this level, it will be difficult to compete with professionals.

>>

CUSTOMIZATION
SKILL

Finishing Color Mixing
The Undercoat and Paint Tone Create the Air Jordan–Like Look

The final red is "toned" using multiple Angelus Paints. Angelus Paint, which specializes in sneakers, features a lineup that reproduces the colors of well-known sneakers, but there are subtle differences in the finished product depending on the compatibility with the base coat. Of course, for standard finishes, there is no problem using Angelus Paint as is. However, in the world of professionals, there is always that "next step."

13 Use a watercolor palette when mixing Angelus Paints. This customization uses standard RED as a base color and adds a small amount of FLATWHITE and VARSITY—a collector's-edition paint with a more sneaker-like color scheme.

14 It is possible to quantify this recipe, but in many cases, the coloration differs between the paint as it is and after it has dried. So, we recommend you test-paint a piece of leather first. Then, check the color once it dries, and fine-tune it to your liking. If you are checking the color on a test piece of leather, don't forget to apply the base coat and then add your color(s).

15 After mixing the Angelus Paint, it's time to apply it over the base color. As you can see, no masking tape is used here. That is only because the customizer has done many projects and is very used to this process. If you are unfamiliar with this process yourself, you may feel less pressure if you apply masking tape to the midsole before painting.

16 Here we see the toe cap painted with the mixed color produced in step 13. The color is more magenta than the so-called bright red of the Air Jordan, and it has a certain depth to it. This isn't just red. Rather, it is a reproduction of what fans would associate with the desirable Air Jordan 1's red.

>>

Finish Painting and Allow to Dry
When Mixing Paint, It's Best to Make Plenty

CUSTOMIZATION SKILL

After drying the painted toe cap and checking their coloration, proceed to the next step. The customizer who worked on this project repeated the painting and drying process many times. Depending on the size of the painted surface, he would even use a heat gun to dry the parts before he finished painting the whole thing. It may seem like a process that can be skipped, because it dries naturally without the use of a heat gun, but the heat gun makes a difference in the finished product.

17 Proceed to paint the part where the base coat was applied. The Air Jordan 1 "Bloodline" used in this project has red piping on the parts. So, you don't have to worry about paint protruding a bit here and there. This bonus feature has become widely known among customizers, and its popularity as a base shoe for custom painting is rapidly increasing.

18 Paint and dry the parts in small increments. In this example, we didn't finish painting the entire shoe all at once. We actually applied two coats of paint to each part, which means that the drying process is very important. Drying the parts can be done with a hairdryer, but a heat gun is more efficient because of its higher heat output.

19 Paint the heel in the same way as the other parts. Beginners tend to apply a thick coat of paint in order to avoid having to apply two coats. However, a thick coat will tend to drip, which leads directly to failures and color smudging into neighboring areas. The recovery process from this type of mistake is quite tedious, so applying two thinner coats saves time and effort in the end.

20 After painting the part, let it dry again. This paint job uses a mixed color that is then applied to the entire surface of the chosen parts. If you aren't used to mixing paints to produce the intended color, it is best not to mix any additional paint in the middle of the painting process. This will result in a slightly different color. To avoid any unforeseen problems, make plenty of the desired color at the beginning and just store the excess in small bottles.

>>

Correcting Mistakes and Checking Painted Areas

Meticulous Attention to Detail Gives You a Sense of Satisfaction in the End

CUSTOMIZATION SKILL

After the last coat of paint is applied to the parts in contact with the midsole, and before proceeding with the Jordan Wings logo, it is time to fix any leftover or overflowing paint. It is important to check not only for paint overflow, but also for any unpainted areas on the edges and stitching. If you find an unpainted area where the base black is exposed, apply the Lilac and allow it to dry thoroughly before painting over it.

21 The base Air Jordan 1 "Bloodline" shoes in this example have a section of leather exposed in the gap between the parts and the piping. It is not noticeable when you wear it because it is in the shadows, but you will notice it when you hold the finished product in your hands. We should paint the unpainted section in red.

22 Wipe off any paint that protrudes, using acetone on a cotton pad or melamine sponge. Don't forget to apply masking tape to the painted parts before proceeding, so as not to peel off the paint. Once the paint has been removed, remove the masking tape and check the painted surface again.

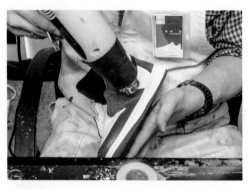

23 After removing the excess paint, apply hot air to the worked area with a heat gun. In reality, acetone dries shortly after it has been wiped off, so it may not be necessary to dry the surface again. However, it is essential for those who aim to improve their painting skills to learn this kind of painting and drying routine.

24 Here, all paint has been wiped off the midsole. The contrast between white and red on the toe area is reminiscent of the Chicago color that sneaker fans adore. Once all the details have been cleaned, it's time to move on to the final challenge of painting the Jordan Wings logo and surrounding areas.

>>

NIKE AIR JORDAN 1 HIGH OG "BLOODLINE"

Paint around the Jordan Wings Logo
Create a Relaxing Work Environment

Let's move on to the most difficult part of the custom-painting process for the Air Jordan 1: the area surrounding the Jordan Wings logo. Since the sneaker is so popular, there is a high demand for Air Jordan 1 custom painting, but many beginners end up losing heart during the Jordan Wings logo- process. There is no "backdoor trick" to this process, and even the customizer who worked on this project had to focus when working on this painstaking process.

25 The Jordan Wings logo is painted using a very fine detail paintbrush, similar to the manner of the base Lilac color. In order to achieve the Chicago color, two coats of the same color must be applied. This is a time-consuming process that is sometimes demotivating for beginners. Unfortunately, there is no other option but to deal with it and learn to progress steadily.

26 Once about half the details have been painted, the surface must be allowed to dry. Then, a second coat is applied and allowed to dry again. Concentration and endurance when repeating the process is the key to success. It is a time-consuming process no matter what, so try using a relaxing environment. Perhaps you can try listening to your favorite music?

27 Painting the letters on the Jordan Wings logo is a particularly nerve-wracking task. The typeface (font) used for the logo is another detail that gives the Air Jordan 1 its unique look. It is absolutely necessary to faithfully trace the typeface embossed on the ankle. It's important to trace the typeface when applying the base coat.

28 Once the inside of the Jordan Wings logo has been painted Red, the area around it is next. At this point some unpainted parts on the heel reinforcement were discovered, so we had to stop with the Red and paint those in the base color. Even professionals can't eliminate oversights. Just remember, it's important not to panic, and to take your time while covering the missing areas.

>>

CUSTOMIZATION SKILL

Finishing Up the Jordan Wings Logo
The Quality of the Pro Store Wings Is Amazing

After fixing the unpainted areas and finishing the area around the Jordan Wings logo, the Jordan Wings logo itself will be finished. The final task involves fine-tuning the details with black paint. In addition to correcting any areas where red paint juts out, add the TM (trademark symbol) next to the logo. This is an iconic part of the Air Jordan 1, so you need to make it as detailed as possible.

29 Use Angelus' Black to fine-tune the Jordan Wings logo. This is a standard color, often used along with white for custom painting of sneakers. So, if you are planning to purchase this product, it is best to use the large-capacity 4-ounce version. Fine-tuning the Jordan Wings logo requires a lot of detail work and thus a very fine detail brush.

30 Use an ultrafine brush for the Jordan Wings logo details. Keep the shape of the embossing in mind and paint only the bottom. On a different note, the stitching that runs horizontally across the heel reinforcement is painted white, just like the original Chicago.

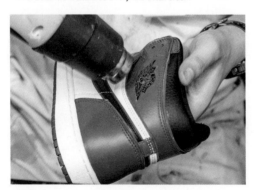

31 After adjusting the logo, dry with a heat gun. This is quite the labor-intensive process, but the feeling of accomplishment when you complete a set of beautifully finished logos is very special. No matting agent was added to the paint, so the glossy surface is noticeable as it is. But don't worry; the gloss will be adjusted with the topcoat at the end.

32 After the Jordan Wings logos have been adjusted, add the "TM" (trademark) symbol. In the hands of a professional, the Jordan Wings logos can be so beautiful. It is difficult for an inexperienced customizer to create highly accurate Jordan Wings logos. Even so, the process is definitely worth the challenge.

>>

Apply Topcoat to the Upper

CUSTOMIZATION SKILL

Chicago-Colored Sneakers with a Little Something Extra

To finish off the process, a topcoat is applied. The topcoat is a finishing agent that protects the painted surface from minor damage and helps maintain the condition of the custom paint. In this case, we will use Matte Acrylic Finisher, which is

available from Angelus Paint. This is the least shiny finish among the current Angelus Paint finishers.

33 When applying Acrylic Finisher by brush, the undiluted solution should be applied directly to the painted surface. When applying the topcoat with an airbrush, be sure to use the special thinner solution Angelus 2-Thin. Dilute to a ratio of about 2:1. The undiluted solution looks thin and cloudy, but it becomes colorless and transparent once dry, so there is no problem.

34 Use a broad brush to apply topcoat treatment to the entire painted surface. In this example, the top-coated and unpainted parts have the same gloss. However, if the gloss is really different from one area to the next, it may be a good idea to apply topcoat to the unpainted parts as well, just to adjust the surface gloss.

35 Once the topcoat is dry, our custom paint job is complete! Of course, in the actual process, not all parts are dried after the topcoat is applied. Rather, small sections of each part are repeatedly dried. Since this is the final step of the surface treatment process, it is important to dry the parts quickly to avoid the risk of dust sticking to the surface.

36 Air Jordan 1 "Bloodline." custom painted to look like the "Chicago." The Jordan Wings logo on the ankle emphasizes the "Chicago" look, and the piping around the parts is an additional detail that gives it a tasteful look.

>>

CUSTOMIZATION SKILL

"Chicago"-Style Customization That Has Become an Instagram Sensation
It's No Wonder That So Many Fans Have Noticed These Custom Sneakers

It is no exaggeration to say that the Air Jordan 1s are the most popular sneakers in the world. This custom paint job was completed with a level of perfection that exceeded our expectations. The piping around the Swoosh, which was not altered at the time of our interview, was later painted black to emphasize the "Chicago" look.

Some fans may prefer the feel of the original "Bloodline" color, but when you see the result of this customization, it's no wonder that they are a hot topic on Instagram. At JUNKYARD Koenji—the

customizer who worked on this project—they will accept orders for custom sneakers, including arranging your own "Bloodline" to look like a "Chicago." Please consult with JUNKYARD Koenji in advance for delivery dates and prices, since they consistently have back orders.

CUSTOMIZER INFORMATION

Junkyard Koenji
Sneakers at Random Koenji Store

3-53-8 Koenji-Minami,
Suginami-ku, Tokyo, Japan 166-0003
Phone: 03-5913-7690

https://sneaker-at-random.com/

Director
Mr. Kidokoro

>>

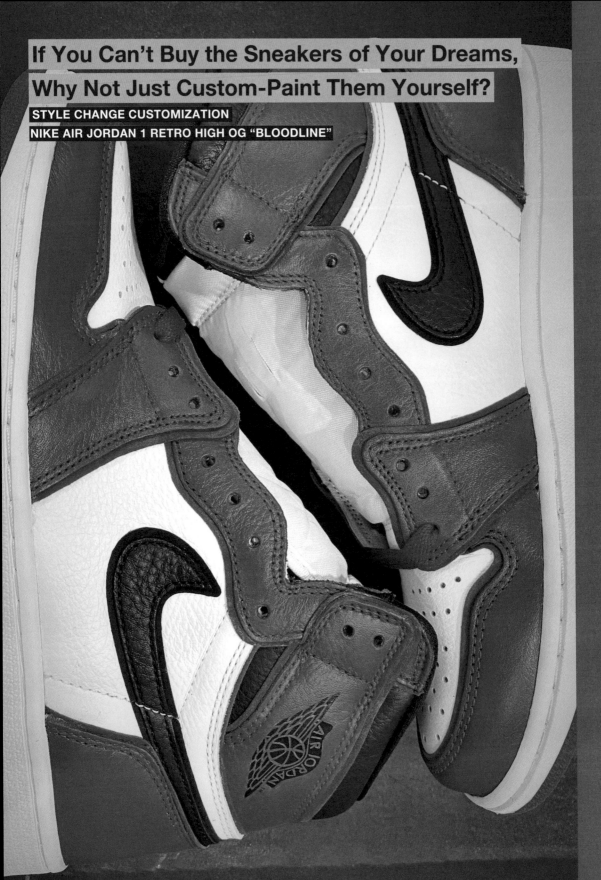

If You Can't Buy the Sneakers of Your Dreams, Why Not Just Custom-Paint Them Yourself?

STYLE CHANGE CUSTOMIZATION
NIKE AIR JORDAN 1 RETRO HIGH OG "BLOODLINE"

CASE STUDY
#08
ONE-POINT REDESIGN

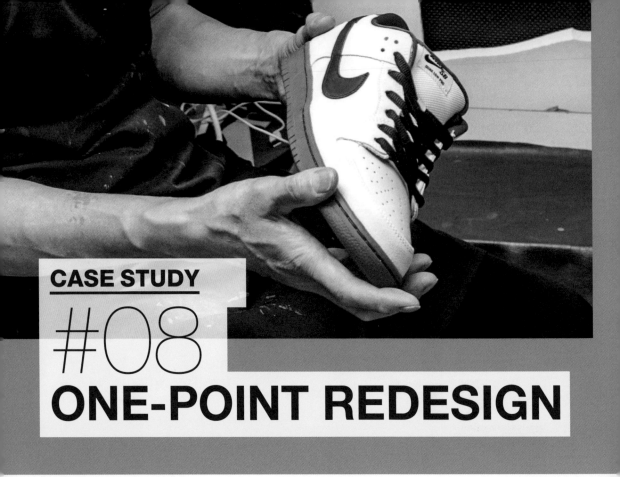

CASE STUDY #08

ONE-POINT REDESIGN >>
NIKE SB DUNK LOW PRO "MUSLIN"

The Iconic Side Panel Swoosh:
Customize by Replacing with Different Materials

SB Dunk is one of the most popular sneaker categories in the modern sneaker scene. Limited-edition collaboration models are especially popular. Even online stores, which use lotteries to determine who can buy the shoes, are overwhelmed. It is very difficult to obtain these highly sought-after sneakers.
Still, if you can't find special Dunks, you can create your own by customizing! Based on this concept, we elected to customize the "Muslin," which are relatively easy to find among Dunks. We will customize the side panel Swoosh.

In Cooperation with Repair Studio AMOR

Start

CUSTOMIZATION SKILL 1

Custom Directions to Consider
Create a One-of-a-Kind Pair of Custom Sneakers

There are two main ways in which sneakers can be customized. You can either take an existing sneaker design and add accents, or you can create a completely new design that has never existed before. The latter is worth the effort, but it is difficult to create the image of the finished product in your mind. In this section, we will take advantage of the well-designed NIKE Dunk and create a custom design that incorporates the "Reverse Swoosh" detail found in some premier models.

01 Check the structure of the sneaker and plan out the process of replacing the Swoosh. In this Dunk, the heel part and the back end of the Swoosh are sewn together. We considered removing the overlapping seam but decided to cut off the overlapping part in order to reduce customization hurdles and to maintain strength.

02 When reversing the Swoosh, it is necessary to change the size for balance reasons. So, it is assumed that the parts will be cut from other leather instead of simply reversing the original Swoosh. If you don't have access to leather, you can buy a used leather bag at a thrift store at a reasonable price.

03 Cut the Swoosh stitches with a sewing tool called a seam ripper. You can use scissors as well, but the seam ripper scoops out the thread and cuts it easily with the blade in the hollow. A simple seam ripper can be purchased at a dollar store. So, go ahead and grab one if you want to try this type of customization.

04 Use thread cutters or scissors to cut anything that cannot be removed by the seam ripper. If you lift the Swoosh, it will be easier to cut the thread. But be careful: if you pull the thread too hard, you might damage the base material. Try to separate all the threads that connect the side panel to the Swoosh, even if you find it tedious.

CUSTOMIZATION SKILL

Parts Removal
Utilize Original Seams as a Design

Remove Swoosh from side panel and check condition of underlying material. The "Reverse Swoosh" custom introduced here assumes that the Swoosh will have a different shape from the original. Therefore, when the custom is complete, some of the base material hidden by the original

Swoosh, as well as the holes made when it was sewn on, will be exposed. The stitching on the side panels is noticeable, but the design of these custom sneakers has been adjusted to make the most of this situation.

05 Here, we are almost finished removing the seam of the Swoosh. In this Dunk, the back edge of the Swoosh passes under the heel tag. You can see that it is not possible to remove the entire Swoosh just by cutting the seam. This structure is often seen in NIKE basketball shoes from the 1980s—often called "old school."

06 We considered removing the seams where the parts overlap, but since resewing requires a certain level of skill, we chose to just cut out the Swoosh along the heel parts so that even beginners could perform this customization. The Swoosh was lifted up and cut out gradually with a precision knife. Take great care not to damage the base material!

07 Here, the Swoosh has been removed from the side panel. Before it was removed, the Swoosh looked like it was simply sewn on the side panel. But upon closer inspection, there were traces of glue on the surface hidden by the Swoosh. It is likely that the Swoosh was fixed with glue before being sewn on during manufacturing. These traces of glue will be removed in a later process, since they ruin the appearance.

08 After cutting off the Swoosh, carefully remove the remaining thread from the side panel with tweezers. Depending on their condition, it may be difficult to remove the threads in some places. The shortcut to success is to proceed steadily without resorting to brute force. We are replacing four Swooshes in this case, so we will proceed with the same process for all four sides.

>>

Removing Adhesive Residue from Upper
Cleaning Methods for Removing Residue Will Vary Depending on Conditions and Materials

The Dunk looked as if the Swoosh was sewn to the side panel, but when the Swoosh was actually removed, we found that a large amount of adhesive residue remained. If we were simply exchanging the Swooshes, there would be no problem, because the glue would be hidden by the replaced Swooshes when finished. In this case, however, where "Reverse Swooshes" are our goal, the glue marks would be exposed. To improve the appearance of the finished product, we recommend removing the adhesive residue by cleaning with the correct method based on the material.

09 The glue marks on the side panels were concentrated at the front and rear edges of the Swoosh. The glue marks have become dark because the Swoosh color has transferred over. Note that the color of the glue may be different from other colors. Also, even if the color isn't noticeable, lumpy glue marks will greatly reduce the quality of the product, so clean everything well.

10 The back end of the Swoosh was particularly stubborn. Use tweezers to forcefully remove the adhesive residue. Then, use a commercially available cleaner (adhesive remover) to clean. Be aware that some cleaners are not suitable for leather! Be sure to check instructions before use.

11 The Dunk "Muslin" upper is made of suede or nubuck material. So, fine grit sandpaper was used to remove the adhesive residue. Sandpaper is not recommended for sneakers with leather uppers because of the high risk of damaging other parts.

12 Here, the side panel with the adhesive residue removed. The cleaning process is complete after we remove the few remaining threads. The rubbery, hardened adhesive was cleaned, but we were not able to remove the marks that had soaked into the material. One way to hide these stains is to paint them the same color as the surrounding area. That being said, it is difficult to reproduce the texture of suede or nubuck.

>>

CUSTOMIZATION
SKILL

Balancing the Replacement Parts
The Shape of the Removed Part Determines the Reverse Swoosh Position

In this "Reverse Swoosh" customization, only the outside Swooshes are reversed. The inside Swooshes are the same design as the original, just with a different material. For the inside, the removed Swoosh can be used as a "template."

However, for the outside, the original Swoosh is too small to be reversed, so a template is created with the size and balance altered. This process requires the most feel, since there are essentially no templates available.

13 Since the purpose of the "Reverse Swoosh" was to rearrange the design, we wanted to create some impact with the completed customization. Therefore, after repeated trial and error—like making enlarged copies of the removed Swooshes—we created a template that is both larger than the removed Swoosh *and* thicker at the curve.

14 Transfer the paper template to the leather scraps and adjust the final balance by actually matching them up with the sneakers. You can kill two birds with one stone by using a piece of leather that is similar in color to the part you are replacing. That way, you can easily check the color balance. If it is difficult to find suitable leather scraps, you can just use colored kraft paper from the dollar store.

15 Once the template for the Swoosh is complete, disassemble the leather bag from which the template will be cut. This time, considering the color of the base model, we purchased a used leather bag, brownish in color, at a local thrift store for about $10. The surface of the leather is stamped with an ostrichlike pattern, which is expected to accentuate the finished look.

16 Place the paper template on the disassembled leather bag and check the position of the Swooshes to be cut out. Synthetic leather can also be used to cut out replacement Swooshes, but be sure to check the condition when buying used synthetic leather. The edges of the synthetic leather may stand out in some cases, and synthetic leather tends to deteriorate much more quickly than genuine leather.

>>

Cutting Out Replacement Swooshes
The Swoosh Design Can Be Made Symmetrical by Reversing the Template

CUSTOMIZATION SKILL

Use the Reverse Swoosh template and transfer it to the back of the leather where the parts will be cut out. A leather-marking pen is used to draw lines on the flesh side of the leather. It's easiest to make a symmetrical stencil by just turning the completed one over as needed, rather than making separate originals. On the other hand, for the inside Swoosh—where the balance doesn't change—it's better to use the removed parts to make a stencil. This will ensure a high level of accuracy.

17 When transferring the template to the flesh side (back), use double-sided tape to prevent it from moving. Be sure to reapply the tape each time. When making templates from thin kraft paper, it is especially important to prepare the templates in a manner such that they can be securely fixed and precisely traced.

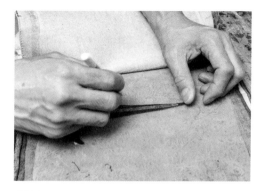

18 Once the template for one shoe is complete, turn it over and trace it for the other shoe. Positioning of the template for cutting should be carefully considered to avoid waste. Especially when cutting parts out of used leather bags, there is a high possibility that the same material with the same texture will never be available again. Use the material effectively to have leftovers that can be used to recover from a mistake.

19 It is a little difficult to see in the photo, but this is what it looks like when the lines have been drawn with a leather-marking pen on the flesh side of the leather. If there is no difference in the size of the parts to be cut out, some distortion of the lines can be corrected during the cutting process. If you really want to correct the lines, you can use a normal eraser (may not work with some types of leather) or a dedicated eraser specifically for the type of pen you used.

20 After transferring the template for the inside Swooshes, roughly cut to shape to make it easier to nicely cut out the parts. Leather scissors can be purchased at handicraft stores and from online stores. Prices vary, but for thin leather, cheap scissors that cost around $10 should work.

>>

CUSTOMIZATION SKILL

Cut Out Custom Parts

Final Confirmation of Balance and Color Coordination

Replacement parts are cut out of the leather from which the template was copied. The design of the Swoosh has many curves. The customizers we interviewed all used scissors to cut out these parts. However, if you are not used to cutting leather, it might be better to use a box cutter, even if it is somewhat troublesome. It is also important to reconfirm the balance of the design during this process, in order to determine if you really like the look. It is really difficult to fix after the parts are installed.

21 Use leather scissors to cut along the marked lines. The customizer at the store explained that it is more beautiful to cut all in one slice whenever possible. This is something that comes only with experience. If you are not familiar with cutting leather, it is probably safer to proceed with caution, using both scissors and a box cutter depending on the design.

22 Match up the cutout Swooshes with the sneakers and check the finished look. The next step is to make sure that the shape and color are exactly as you imagined. If the shape and color are not as you imagined, you may have to stop right here and make new Swooshes.

23 The left and right parts can now be laid out side by side. In this example, there was a concern that the color of the Swoosh would blend in with the surrounding area, resulting in a boring design. But the use of ostrich faux leather accentuates the Swoosh and gives it a more "cohesive" look. The result of this "Reverse Swoosh" custom should be really interesting.

24 Comparing the four Swooshes cut from a used leather bag. The top two Swooshes are for the inside and the bottom two are for the outside. The bottom two must be installed in reverse. You can see here that the size of the original Swooshes appeared weak when reversed. If left as is, the overall balance would have changed significantly.

>>

CUSTOMIZATION SKILL

Preparation for Swoosh Installation

Reproducing the Swoosh Detail That Bites Into the Midsole

The biggest highlight in the "Reverse Swoosh" custom is the detail where part of the Swoosh bites into the midsole. However, removing the stitching from the midsole, inserting the Swoosh, and resewing is not just time consuming, it is also difficult to achieve an aesthetic that is worth the effort. In this section, we will introduce an approach to improve the detail—without removing the stitching—by just modifying some of the newly installed custom Swooshes.

25 Recheck the balance by placing one of the Reverse Swooshes in position. The depth of the overlap into the midsole is about 2 cm / ¾". Since that much overlap requires removing stitches on the midsole and then sewing it back together, we have decided to cut off part of the Swoosh instead. This will create the intended look where part of the Swoosh goes under the midsole.

26 Mark the midsole line on the Swoosh. In this case, a leather-marking pen was used since the Swoosh is quite dark. However, if it was much lighter, you could use an erasable gel pen. The ink in these pens turns transparent at temperatures above 60 degrees Celsius and can thus be cleanly erased with a heat gun.

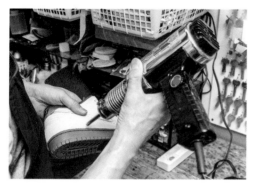

27 The stitching is left in place at this point, but the midsole adhesive is peeled off where the Swoosh crosses into it. The first step is to heat the parts with a heat gun to soften the glue. It's easier to proceed with this process if you have a nozzle that can concentrate the hot air.

28 Once heat has been applied and the glue has softened, insert a flathead screwdriver behind the midsole to create a gap. If you are using brand-new sneakers, the adhesive will be very strong, and it will take a lot of effort just to make a gap. If you try to pry them open forcefully, you will damage the surrounding material, so be careful and constantly check the condition of the shoe as you go.

>>

Fine-Tuning the Swooshes

CUSTOMIZATION SKILL

Adjust Thickness of the Swooshes Where They Go behind the Midsole to Improve Appearance

Once the gap into the midsole is set, you have to insert the Swoosh to check the finish. As far as we could tell, we could just continue by slicing off a part of the Swoosh. Also, the expert at the store decided that it would be better to adjust the thickness of the part where the Swoosh comes

in close contact with the midsole. That way it would fit into the midsole gap better and be less noticeable. That would produce a much more beautiful finish. In this section, the Swooshes will be fine-tuned to improve both efficiency and finish.

29 Using the marked line drawn on the Swoosh in the previous step as a reference, cut off the part of the Swoosh. Leave a few millimeters below the marked line that can be embedded under the midsole. Use a stainless-steel ruler and a leather craft tool called a "skiving knife." If the material is already fairly thin, a utility knife can be used instead.

30 After adjusting the Swoosh so that it will embed into the midsole correctly, insert the Swoosh part that goes under the midsole into the gap. It is possible to proceed with the work as is, but the thickness of the leather may cause a bump and affect a final result. Here, we will put in a little extra work so that the finished product will be more beautiful.

31 Use a skiving knife to carve leather from the backside of the Swoosh. Correct any bumps so that they become as inconspicuous as possible. It's difficult to do this work with a box cutter, and even if you have a skiving knife, some skill is required. When using a skiving knife, it is best to try it out on an unused piece of leather to get a feel for it before proceeding.

32 Insert the adjusted part of the Swoosh into the midsole and check everything again. It's hard to tell from the photo, but the difference in the part where the Swoosh was inserted is no longer noticeable, and the process of inserting the part of the Swoosh itself has become smoother. Putting in a little extra effort makes things more efficient and increases the beauty of the finished product.

>>

Stitching Custom Swooshes
Making the "Reverse Swoosh" Customization Easier with a Change of Thinking

When performing a custom Swoosh replacement, you might think that since the Swoosh was originally sewn on, it should be sewn on again. However, if you want to keep the original detail, you need to remove the lining of the sneaker so that the seam isn't visible. This is a very difficult process.

However, if you think of customizing sneakers as more of a hobby, you can greatly reduce the difficulty of this problem. All you have to do is to glue on Swooshes with stitching already added to them.

33 First, we need to select stitching thread. In this case we chose brown, the same color as the base. You may be worried about the strength when just gluing the Swoosh. But as you can see from the fact that adhesives are generally used to bond the upper to the sole—the part of the shoe that requires the most strength—you don't have to worry. As long as the Swoosh is glued on correctly with sneaker adhesive, it will be fine.

34 This time we will use a patcher sewing machine to add the stitching to the Swoosh. Unlike a regular sewing machine, a patcher sewing machine can sew in all directions. It is an indispensable item for sewing complex-shaped sneakers and parts. It is an industrial sewing machine that is admired and often used by highly skilled customizers.

35 Stitching can be performed exceptionally well with a patcher sewing machine. If you don't have one, hand stitching is technically acceptable, of course, but it will take a little longer. Here, we used a thread color that was very similar to the custom Swoosh. However, if you want the stitching to be a beautiful accent, it is always interesting to choose a thread color that is different from the base.

36 Outside Swoosh with stitching. The advantage of using a patcher sewing machine is that the stitches are all evenly spaced. The purpose here is to apply decorative stitches, not strength. So, the stitches that would be embedded in the midsole are omitted. The opposite Swoosh is stitched in the same way.

>>

CUSTOMIZATION SKILL 10

Stitching Custom Swooshes
Prepping Swooshes That Will Be Attached to the Medial Side

The medial Swoosh is also stitched in advance, in anticipation of being attached with adhesive. You could always leave the stitching off for design reasons, but for old-school sneakers like the Dunk, the stitching on the parts is an iconic part of the design. You should always try to proactively incorporate any processes like these. They are worth the effort and will surely increase the level of satisfaction in your custom sneakers.

37 The medial Swoosh cut from the leather bag is aligned with the side panel. The shape, length, and color scheme need to be rechecked at this point. In this example, the back end of the Swoosh is not embedded in the heel; rather, it is glued so that the parts adhere to each other. This means that the size of the back end of the Swoosh needs to be carefully adjusted.

38 The medial Swoosh was cut a little longer than it needed to be, because the length can always be adjusted at the end of this process. Align the Swoosh with the sneaker contours and mark a line with a leather-marking pen to match the heel. The joint line is slightly curved, so it is best to use leather scissors to cut off the excess, rather than a skiving knife.

39 The medial Swooshes are also stitched with a patcher sewing machine. Patcher sewing machines aren't particularly affordable because they tend to be reserved for professionals.

40 Here is the medial Swoosh stitching. The curve of the Swoosh and the curve of the stitching match. The back edge, where the Swoosh meets the heel, isn't stitched. This creates the illusion of overlapping. Stitch the other medial Swoosh in the same way, and you're ready to go.

>>

Attaching Custom Swooshes

CUSTOMIZATION SKILL

An Erasable Gel Pen Is Useful for Checking Mounting Positions

Once the custom Swooshes are complete, it's time to check the mounting position. For the medial side, where the custom Swooshes will be attached at the same position as the original Swoosh, the stitching holes left on the side panels can be used as a guideline. However, for the lateral side, where the Swoosh will be reversed, it is difficult to use the stitching holes as a reference. If the left and right sides are unbalanced, it will really throw off the appearance. So, use an erasable gel pen here—a trusted tool for leather craft enthusiasts—to meticulously check positioning.

41 The stitching on the four Swooshes is complete. The embossed faux ostrich leather adds a beautiful accent. In the example shown here, all the Swooshes are the same color, but an interesting effect would be produced if the colors and materials for the medial side and lateral side were changed.

42 Insert the Swooshes into the midsole gaps to secure them. In our "Reverse Swoosh" custom, some of the original stitching holes are exposed when finished. But that just emphasizes the custom sneaker style. In recent years, it is not uncommon to see commercial models with the stitching holes exposed in order to emulate custom sneakers.

43 After deciding where to apply the Reverse Swoosh, use an erasable gel pen to outline it. Leather crafters love to use erasable gel pens because the ink disappears when heated to 60 degrees or more with a heat gun—regardless of the type of leather.

44 The lateral side upper has been outlined with an erasable gel pen. Do the same for the Swoosh that will be mounted on the medial side. This is to prepare for gluing. We will use the outline as a reference when applying primer or adhesive and when gluing the Swooshes on the upper.

>>

CUSTOMIZATION SKILL 12

Surface Preparation with Primer
Don't Forget to Sand the Target Surface

After determining the positioning, apply primer to both the sneaker body and the Swooshes. The choice of primer depends on the adhesive used, so be sure to check the instructions of the adhesive when you buy it. If you apply the primer evenly to the surface and allow it to dry, the "bite" of the adhesive will be greatly improved. This is an essential step for your custom sneakers.

45 Apply primer to backsides of the Swooshes with a (fine tip) brush. Be careful not to leave any residue on the edges of the Swooshes, since it will tend to peel off. Some primers on the market have a brush attached to the back of the lid for application. This can be an advantage for beginners since it eliminates the need for solvents to clean the brush after applying the primer.

46 After applying the primer, allow it to dry in a clean, dust-free environment. There are some types of sneaker adhesives that do not require primer, but even with these types, the strength will not decrease with primer. So really, applying primer is our best choice.

47 Use the primer drying time to sandpaper the surface of the sneaker body. Although it is not necessary to sand suede parts, sanding leather and short nubuck material will improve primer and glue adhesion. Even if it is tedious, it is worth the effort.

48 After the sandpaper treatment is complete, remove dust with a brush and apply primer to the inside of the outline. The primer was applied all at once with a rather thick brush. Note that if any areas protrude, they will be very noticeable once they have dried. So, use a thin brush and carefully apply the primer until you get used to it.

CUSTOMIZATION SKILL

Gluing On Swoosh (Medial Side)
Take Your Time and Apply Adhesive Carefully

Once the primer is dry, apply adhesive to the sneakers. There are many different types of adhesives available for sneakers, but the ones that are strong enough and durable enough to be used for soles are generally pressure-bonded after drying. There are also types that can be used immediately after the primer has dried, and types that are used after heating the surface with a heat gun. Before you proceed, be sure to choose the one that is best for your needs.

49 Apply sneaker glue to the entire target surface, as if painting over the dried primer. The Swoosh will be glued together after the glue dries, so there is no need to worry about time, like with instant adhesives. It is more efficient to apply the adhesive to all the Swooshes instead of going one by one.

50 Apply the glue carefully so that it doesn't protrude from the edges of the target surface. The customizer used cotton swabs to work on small areas. Disposable cotton swabs are more efficient because there is no need to clean them afterward. If you are not confident in your ability to work with cotton swabs, you can use a brush from a dollar store. Although that may be a bit wasteful.

51 After the glue that has been applied to the sneaker body and the Swoosh has dried, it's time to put everything together. Once the glue doesn't stick when you touch it with your finger, you are ready to start attaching the Swoosh. There is no right answer as to whether the front or back end of the Swoosh should be attached first; just go with the order that makes you most comfortable.

52 Here is the medial Swoosh in position. If the Swooshes can be tightly pressure-bonded, without floating, it should help them appear as though they were sewn on with thread. If we were to actually sew on the Swooshes, we would need much more time and effort. Once you see the finished product, you'll realize that sewing isn't the only correct option.

Gluing Swoosh (Lateral Side)

CUSTOMIZATION SKILL

If the Prep Is Perfect, Applying the Swoosh Should Go Smoothly

Once the medial Swoosh is complete, the Reverse Swoosh can be attached. This is the key to our customization, but the basic flow is the same as for the medial side. The only difference is that a portion of Swoosh is inserted into the midsole. If the left and right positioning is correct and primer and glue are perfect, you shouldn't experience any trouble with this process. Try not to get too excited, and just carefully glue parts together.

53 After the glue that has been applied to the sneaker body and Swoosh has dried, it is time to apply the Reverse Swoosh. First, use a flathead screwdriver or similar tool to widen the gap where the Swoosh will be inserted into the midsole. Then, insert the Reverse Swoosh. Be careful to press only on the area that needs to be inserted at this point.

54 The Reverse Swoosh has been applied to the sneaker body. The contrast between the original stitching holes and the Reverse Swoosh emphasizes the custom look. The lines of the erasable gel pen used as a guide can be completely erased by heating with a heat gun.

55 After attaching the Reverse Swoosh, use a gouge, scriber, or dull mini chisel to fill the gaps between the midsole and the Swooshes with adhesive. This step reduces the risk of unwanted gaps when the sneaker is actually worn. This important step cannot be avoided. It makes sneakers that not only look good but are also fun to wear.

56 Checking the balance after the customization is finished. If the Swoosh is misaligned at this stage, it can be removed by heating with a heat gun. One of the advantages of the glued-on Reverse Swoosh customization is that it is easier to fix mistakes when compared to actually sewing on the Swooshes.

>>

Complete

CUSTOMIZATION SKILL 15

Completed Reverse Swoosh Custom
One-of-a-Kind Sneakers with Popular Details That Anyone Could Recognize

Sneakers with a Reverse Swoosh have an overwhelming presence on the streets. The pair shown here is sure to turn heads of many sneaker fans when worn on the streets. The fact that this popular detail was made into a custom recipe that anyone can enjoy by gluing parts together must have been a novelty for custom sneaker enthusiasts. Repair Studio Amor, a well-known sneaker repair store, is also a reliable store for custom sneakers.

CUSTOMIZER INFORMATION

Repair Studio Amor

1-1-9, Chijo-Taibai, Wakaba-ku,
Chiba-shi, Chiba, Japan 264-0005
Phone: 043-309-4017

Owner
Mr. Takemoto

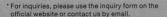

http://www.rs-amor.sakura.ne.jp/

* For inquiries, please use the inquiry form on the
official website or contact us by email.

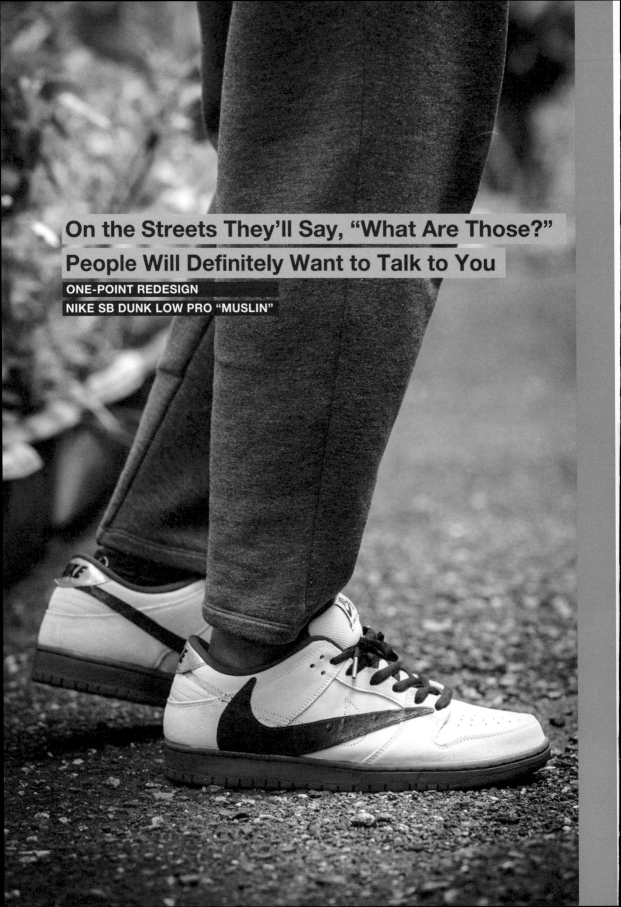

On the Streets They'll Say, "What Are Those?"
People Will Definitely Want to Talk to You

ONE-POINT REDESIGN
NIKE SB DUNK LOW PRO "MUSLIN"

#09
ALL-UPPER
CUSTOM

CASE STUDY
#09
ALL-UPPER CUSTOMIZING

CASE STUDY #09

ALL-UPPER CUSTOMIZING >>
NIKE AIR FORCE 1 LOW

This Pair of Sneakers Definitely Can't Be Purchased Commercially

NIKE also offers "Bespoke," a service that allows you to choose the color and material of the upper, and once the design has been made it cannot be reordered. However, this service is currently available only in limited stores, and it is not the easiest to order. What makes this possible is the "All Upper" method, where the upper of the sneaker is made from commercially available leather. In this chapter, I will interview a customizer who is active on Instagram and report on the production process of this ultimate sneaker customization, the "All Upper."

In Cooperation with: @ch500usmade

Start

CUSTOMIZATION SKILL

Dismantling Sneakers to Use as Patterns

Dismantle the Upper of the Same Model and Make Patterns

The ultimate in customization, "All Uppers" are created by redesigning the upper of the sneaker itself. Once the customization is fixed in your mind, the process starts with cutting parts from the chosen material. There are no official stencils available from sneaker brands, so you have to make your own. Here, we will dismantle a low-cut Air Force 1 and make the paper patterns necessary for customization.

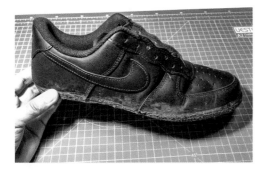

01 For this example, it is best to prepare a low-cut Air Force 1 with the sole unit already removed. In order to make patterns for All Uppers, you need to have not only the model, but also the same upper as the finished size. NIKE and other manufacturers adjust the balance of their parts based on size.

02 Paint the upper with sneaker paint so that you can see where the parts overlap even when disassembled. In this case, white paint was used because the base color is black. There is no need to paint carefully, since this is just a guideline for putting the parts together. However, make sure to color the boundaries between the parts.

03 The insole sewn to the upper is removed with a precision knife by cutting through the stitching. The sneakers do not have to be new, but if they are wrinkled from use, there is a risk that they will be distorted when transferring the pattern. It is a bit of a waste, but it's wise to use uppers that are in good condition.

04 The original parts around the heel that were hidden in the disassembled Air Force 1 Swoosh looked like a single piece from the outside. But when actually disassembled, it turns out that the parts were divided into upper and lower and sewn together. It was decided that there would be no problem if this part was replaced with a single piece, so the detail surrounding the part division in the stencil was omitted.

CUSTOMIZATION SKILL

Making Paper Patterns for the Upper
Transfer the Patterns from the Dismantled Parts, Including the Stitching Holes

Since there are no official stencils available, the only way to make templates for our All Uppers is to make them ourselves. Not surprisingly, there are several custom sneaker brands that sell paper patterns. Some of them also sell acrylic patterns that can withstand repeated use, but we were not able to verify the copyright of these products, so please use you own judgment when purchasing them for your customizations.

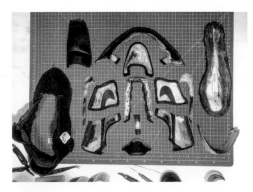

05 The upper has been disassembled. Out of the fifteen parts, the shoes and lining will require a separate process, so let's start with the original pattern for the toe box, heel parts, and other parts to be cut out of leather.

06 Place the disassembled parts on a piece of cardboard and use a fine-tipped pen to outline the patterns. Although simple drawing paper can be used, it is wise to use more-durable paper, since the pattern will be used over and over.

07 Push an awl through the seams to make holes in the pattern. It may not be necessary to sew the parts with the same stitch width as the originals, but the stitching on the upper is iconic and gives the sneakers that old-school look. It is a good idea to record the stitching positions on the pattern so that they can be used later on.

08 Here, the details of the part have been copied onto the pattern. After this, cut out the cardboard along the outline to complete the pattern for this part. The stitching holes made with the awl are connected, and the pattern paper is cut out thinly to form a guideline.

>>

CUSTOMIZATION SKILL

Transfer the Pattern to the Leather That Will Form the Parts

Color Coordination of the Parts Is Where We Show Off Aesthetic Taste

Once the pattern is ready, lay it out on the material and transfer the individual details. This project will use a snakeskin-style stamped leather that exudes a sense of luxury. That will be combined with navy and yellow to create a vivid, coordinated look. Shades also affect the overall impression of the finished product, so we selected a dark-blue, almost black, leather material. The result is a custom sneaker with a bold yet chic look.

09 Once the color scheme for the upper has been decided on, lay out the pattern on the material. In this example, the toe guard, Swoosh, parts around the heel, and eyestays will be finished in navy. In order to minimize the number of scraps, the patterns will need to be adjusted a few times.

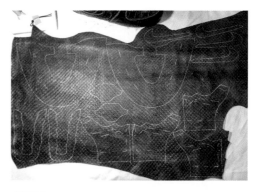

10 The navy leather was marked with a leather-marking pen to create patterns for both feet. Since the medial and lateral heel parts need to be symmetrical for each foot, a total of four stencils were made for the front and back. Use the leather-marking pen to draw a line around the part joints. This will be used as a guideline for matching up the parts later.

11 In this customization, yellow parts will be used for the toe box and side panels to create a vivid contrast on the upper. The paper pattern is lined up on the yellow stamped leather and outlined with a leather-marking pen or an erasable gel pen. The customizer we interviewed was using Schreibger's "Schneider K1."

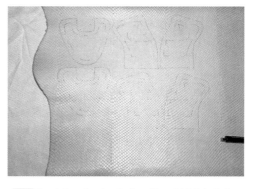

12 Here is the yellow faux leather with part details for both feet laid out. Six pieces will be cut from this material, but we need to use only two patterns. The patterns for all uppers are used quite a bit and get damaged quickly. So, it is a good idea to make copies of the patterns when you're done, so you can duplicate them as needed.

>>

Cut Out Parts and Attach Temporarily

Use a Natural-Rubber Adhesive to Get an Idea of the Finished Product

After copying the pattern onto the leather, proceed to cut out the parts and temporarily attach them. You can use leather craft scissors or a leather knife to cut out the parts, but if your sneaker has curved parts, you will probably need to use scissors.

Depending on the design, the edges of the parts may be exposed once they are attached to the shoe. So, it is best to have a commercial scissor sharpener on hand to maintain sharpness and thus keep the raw edges crisp.

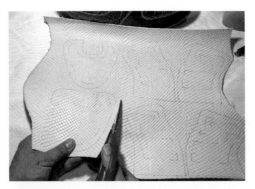

13 Cut out the parts. Don't cut directly on the pattern lines; just roughly cut them out while leaving a margin. Then, cut neatly along the lines. These steps are basic to leather crafting and probably don't need to be explained to customizers, like you, who wish to take up this All Upper challenge.

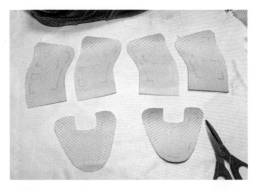

14 The yellow parts for both shoes have now been cut out. A small amount of error can be tolerated here in the interest of "taste." However, if the left and right parts are shaped too differently, there will be undue distortion in the finished product. If there is anything that needs to be corrected, it should be done at this stage. After cutting out the navy parts, let's temporarily attach them.

15 Use the guidelines on the parts to help temporarily fix the cutout parts in the correct positions. Use Kraft's "Leather Tool Rubber Glue" (or something similar like Elmer's Craftbond Multi-Purpose Spray Adhesive, Fiebing's Leathercraft Cement, etc.) for this step. Kraft Rubber Glue is known for its low adhesive strength, which is perfect for temporarily attaching leather parts. It is available at home improvement stores and on Amazon and is also reasonably priced.

16 Use a spatula to spread a thin layer of Kraft Rubber Glue (or equivalent) on both target pieces. If you want to achieve a greater level of adhesion, you can sandpaper the surfaces, but since this is just a temporary fix, it is best to just apply the glue without any pretreatment. We will want better adhesion later in this process, and for that it is recommended that we use a special sneaker adhesive.

>>

Temporarily Attaching Parts for the Upper
Use Core Material to Guarantee Strength

After the parts are fixed temporarily, the "core material" for inserting between the upper and the lining is produced. This material is used as a backer for the upper and has the advantage of being thinner and softer than the leather used in commercial sneakers. That's what makes it useful in custom sneakers. This core material isn't found in most commercial sneakers, but it is essential to realize that it is there when choosing leather material for your custom design.

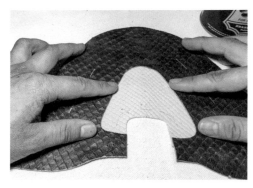

17 The parts coated with rubber glue are pasted together to temporarily form the upper. In this example, materials with different sizes of faux details were selected. When the parts are put together, you can see the contrast between the different details, as well as the color. This is the type of idea that only an experienced customizer can offer.

18 Next, the parts from the toe to the side of the heel will be temporarily attached. The Swoosh on the side panel isn't attached yet, but you can see the overall color coordination. After the same process is done for the other foot, we can start making the "core material" to be inserted between the upper and the lining.

19 In the example shown here, split leather is used as the core material. Split leather is leather where the grain-side surface has been removed. While it is a bit thick, it can be purchased at a reasonable price. Some craft stores that specialize in leather products also sell split leather with resin or film applied to them to increase strength.

20 Place the temporarily fixed parts on the split leather and use a leather-marking pen to trace. The core won't be exposed above the surface of the sneaker, but if it is distorted when the design is transferred, there is a risk that sections of the sneaker will not be strong enough when finished. Don't forget to hold the parts firmly with one hand as you trace the lines, to prevent them from shifting.

CUSTOMIZATION SKILL

Adding the Overlaces
These Popular Details Create Accents in the Design

The main feature of this customization is the overlaces. Overlaces are a second set of shoelaces placed over top of the original laces, a detail that has been previously used in some outdoor shoes. The NIKE × Off-White, which incorporated overlaces into a street sneaker, attracted a lot of attention and became a hot topic in 2019.

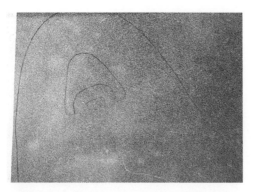

21 After transferring the general outline of the upper, transfer the shape of the toe box, using the pattern. This needs to be done in order to cut out the toe box from the split leather (see #48 for finished look). Doing this helps prevent the material from becoming too thick and compromising the wearability after attaching the interlining material. Once this step is complete, put the interlining production on hold and proceed to making the overlacing system.

22 Add eyelets and loops for overlaces to the upper. In order to determine the correct position for the laces, they were placed on another set of Air Force 1s, and the eyelets were fixed with masking tape. The rope-style laces are a must-have item if the design is to be reminiscent of the NIKE × Off-White model.

23 Once the positions for the eyelets have been determined, draw dots on the masking tape with a marker. At the same time, transfer the joining lines of the surrounding sections to the masking tape. If the design allows, set the eyelets where the upper parts do not overlap, since the material may be thicker, and it may be difficult to make holes.

24 Peel off the masking tape on which the eyelets and joint lines were drawn, and reattach it to the parts being made for the All Upper. At this point, the joint lines on the masking tape will serve as guidelines for reattaching the parts. For this project, we will be making a total of eight overlace eyelets for each shoe.

>>

CUSTOMIZATION SKILL

Punch Eyelets for Overlaces

It's Easy to Do with Specialty Tools

Once you've decided where you want to make the eyelets for the overlaces, use a rotary leather punch—available at home improvement stores or on Amazon—to make holes in the parts. It is possible to make holes without using the rotary leather punch, but the cross section of the holes is sharper with this specialty tool. Another bonus is that it is very easy to make multiple holes of the same size. Furthermore, the tool itself is relatively inexpensive. There is no reason not to use it for this All Upper customization.

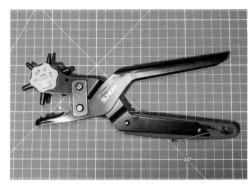

25 The SUNDRY brand rotary leather punch was used by the customizer in charge of this project. Even though the hole positions can be somewhat limited, it is an excellent product that can easily punch holes of six different sizes with its rotating punch blade. Another bonus is that it is relatively inexpensive at around $10–$20 online.

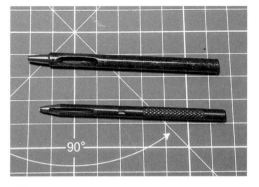

26 Here we have a set of single "punches," trusted tools for leatherworking. These are great tools that can be used to make precise eyelets. Place the leather on a cutting mat, apply the desired diameter punch to the surface, and strike with a rubber hammer to make beautiful and precise eyelets. A set of punches with several different diameters can be purchased for just a couple of dollars.

27 In this example, we will use a rotary leather punch to make eyelets with a diameter of 4 mm / ⅛". Don't forget to use the rotary leather punch after the masking tape marked with the awl has been removed, instead of making the eyelets with the masking tape still attached. Use the punched awl holes as a guide. This step will improve accuracy.

28 Here are the leather parts with the eyelets punched. The structure of rotary leather punch makes it difficult to punch holes directly in the center of the part. When using this type of punch, be sure to have a single punch ready off to the side. Use it if you notice that you can't reach the punch position with the rotary punch or if the leather folds up, for instance.

>>

Attach Grommets to the Eyelets

Grommets Make Amazing Design Accents

Metal grommets are attached to the overlace eyelets. These eyelets are not subjected to a great deal of stress when finished, but since they are usually used on outdoor shoes, grommets are a good design detail to create a tough impression.

Here, silver-colored dovetails with an inner diameter of 4 mm / ⅛" are attached to the leather parts, using a special grommet tool set and base or a set of grommet pliers.

29 We will be using "single-sided grommets" with an inner diameter of 4 mm. The package also shows the outer diameter (8 mm ¼" in this case), but the basic rule is to match up with the inner diameter. In addition to the silver, we see that there are black and gold pieces available. It is often a good idea to choose a color that stands out and creates a distinct accent.

30 With single-sided grommets, we need to insert the convex portion through the surface of the leather and crimp the ring-shaped part from the back. If the front and back are installed incorrectly, it will look like something you would see on the "back side" of the shoe. Use "double-sided grommets" if you want to avoid this problem and have both the front and back look the same.

31 Apply the grommet tool to the backside and strike with a hammer to crimp. The tool used here is for 8 mm / ¼" outer diameter and 4 mm / ⅛" inner diameter. There is also a plier punch for attaching the grommets, but it is necessary to match the grommet sizes.

32 One set of grommets has been attached. After confirming the color coordination, let's attach grommets to the remaining eyelets. This is a simple and quick process, but the finished product is a beautiful set of metal grommets used for outdoor shoes. This is a detail that would look great on any sneaker customization.

>>

Make Ventilation Holes in the Toe Box
Essential for Creating Comfortable Old-School Shoes

CUSTOMIZATION SKILL

Ventilation holes are cut out of the toe cap to create an old-school look. This detail vents moisture that tends to be trapped inside the shoe. It is an essential process to complete a custom sneaker that not only looks retro but is also very comfortable. We cut out the toe box part of the previously made core material to ensure air flow.

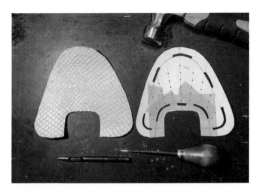

33 The pattern from before is used as a guide for marking ventilation holes in the toe box. For this process, all you need are the cutout parts, the pattern, a punch, a hammer, an awl, and a cutting mat. The position of the ventilation hole on the disassembled Air Force 1 is copied onto the pattern, and those positions are used as a reference.

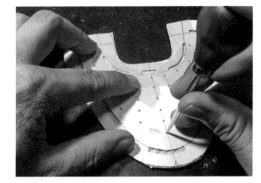

34 Lay the pattern over the toe box and position it so that the ventilation holes can be copied over. Hole positions don't have to be the exact same as the original. Also, note that the arrangement of the holes often differs from model to model. The toe holes can act as a "sneaker fingerprint," so following the original may help you feel more comfortable with the finished product.

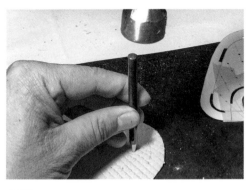

35 After copying the positions of the ventilation holes, use an awl to make the initial holes. Place the punch on the marks made with the awl and strike with a hammer. The diameter of the punches used here should be around 1.5 mm to 2 mm ($^1/_{16}$"). The customizer we interviewed used a larger 2.1 mm ($^1/_{16}$") punch.

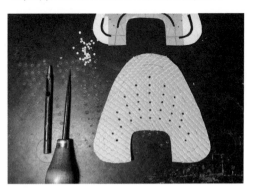

36 The ventilation holes have been made in the toe box. The appearance of the finished product will depend heavily on how beautifully the ventilation holes are arranged in a radial pattern. This is where the customizer shows off his or her skills. Finish making the ventilation holes in the remaining part.

>>

Creating the Overlace Loops
It's the Details That Make the Overlaces Stand Out

Once the toe box pieces are ready, it is time to attach the loops for the overlaces to the grommets. For this All Upper customization, the laces are usually threaded through the eyelets (lace holes). The approach of placing loops on the toe

caps themselves is rare. However, learning new techniques is great because you will always have access to more ideas.

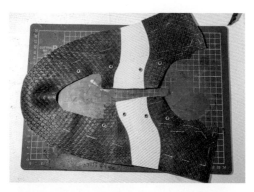

37 In this example, loops will be placed on eight grommets on each side. Since this is a detail that will be exposed on the surface when the project is completed—and it is difficult to replace later –it is necessary to carefully consider the thickness and color of the cord for the loops. In this case, we used black nylon cord for the base.

38 Use an appropriately sized coin to draw patterns for the loop-backing pieces on a piece of leather. There is no need to cut perfect circles, since these parts will be almost hidden when the project is complete. It is best to just pick a size and make sure that all of the pieces are the same. Pay attention here: if you use bright leather, it will stand out behind the grommets, so it is best to select a dark color.

39 Cut out the loop backers with leather scissors and make holes for the cord, using a punch or an awl. In this case, one hole of about 2 mm in the center of the loop backers and two holes about 1 mm above and below that were made. The diameter of the holes needs to be adjusted according to the thickness of the cord, so we recommended checking the size of the holes with a test piece before making holes in everything.

40 Thread the cord so that a loop is formed in the middle hole on the flesh side (backside). Here, nylon cord (about 1 mm (1/16") thick), which is sold as an accessory and easily available at handicraft stores and online stores, was used. Once the loop is ready, glue down the base of the loop where it touches the leather parts (where the cords cross).

>>

Attach Loops for Overlaces
Use Both Sewing and Gluing to Streamline the Process

Once the loops are ready, it is time to attach them to the leather parts that make up the upper. When attaching the loops, it is necessary to choose between "sewing" and "gluing." Sewing is the best choice for areas that require high strength, while gluing is best for areas where you don't want the

stitches to show on the surface of your sneakers. Sewing should be performed with a patcher sewing machine if possible. It really is a favorite of not only sneaker customizers but also many other leather crafters.

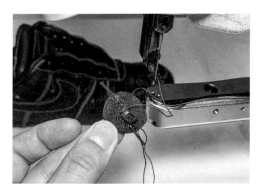

41 The nylon cord is sewn to the leather parts by using a patcher sewing machine, which can sew in all directions. This process can be done by hand, but it requires a ton of work. For All Upper customization, there will be a lot of leather sewing. So, it is no exaggeration to say that an expensive patcher sewing machine is almost essential.

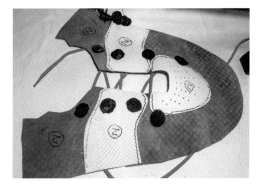

42 Flip over the upper and align the parts with the nylon cords fixed to them with the upper grommets. Pull the loops through the grommets and run the rope lacing through the cords to make it easier to align everything. Once you have decided on the positioning, draw an outline of the upper with a marker. This will serve as a guideline for the area to be glued. Repeat the same process for the other shoe.

43 Apply adhesive to both the upper and the loop backer and attach the loop backer to the upper. When gluing our leather parts together, it is best to create the strongest bond possible by gluing the flesh side (backside) of the leather, rather than the grain side, to the target area. When we made the parts, we made sure that the loops would be on the flesh side in anticipation of this very fact.

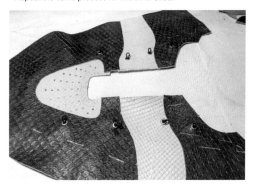

44 The lace loops are attached to all the grommets on the upper. If you put the bright rope laces through these loops, you can re-create the "overlaces" used in the NIKE × Off-White sneakers. It is a unique detail that doesn't go well with all sneakers. Still, we can't wait to see how it looks when they are finished.

>>

Lamination of Leather Parts for the Upper and Core Material

Improves the Overall Strength of the Sneaker, While Also Affecting Comfort

After the loops have been glued down, it is time to proceed with the process of attaching the core material—cut from the split leather—to the upper. The purpose of this process is to strengthen the two pieces of leather so they won't lose their shape when worn. If you use thick leather—like that normally used in commercially available sneakers—there is no need for core material. However, thick leather doesn't come in a wide variety of colors and surface finishes, which limits your design options.

45 Leather parts for the upper and the core material, cut from the split leather, need to be lined up. While the upper parts are made by joining three sections (toe, side panel, and heel) together, the core material is cut from a single piece of split leather from toe to heel. The toe box part of the core material is hollowed out to allow moisture to escape from the ventilation holes.

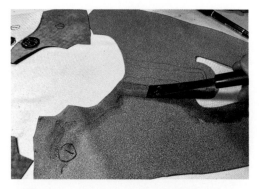

46 Use a spatula to apply rubber cement to both the leather parts and the core material, then paste them together. Given that the parts will be sewn together later, there is no problem using rubber cement that won't create a strong bond. At this stage the cement only has to be strong enough to keep the parts from shifting.

47 We have finished bonding the upper leather parts and the core material. It is nice to see that wrinkles are reduced, and the surface appears to be strong. At this stage, the core material for the shoe tongue is exposed. It will be cut out after the eyestays (shoelace holes) are attached, so let's not worry about it right now.

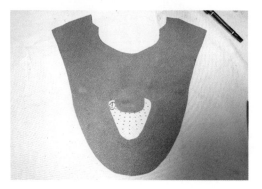

48 Here is a photo of the back of the upper surface and core laminated together. The ventilation holes in the toe box are exposed, which is correct. During this process, the parts for the overlaces attached to the upper are buried between the materials. If the parts are misaligned during the lamination process, just be sure to fix them quickly before the glue dries.

>>

Sewing on the Side Panels and Toe Box
Sew Parts Together with the Same Double Stitching as the Original

After the upper parts and core material are glued together, the side panels and toe caps can be sewn. The reason why only a portion of the parts are sewn together here is because the stitch edges on the side panels and toe box are hidden under the eyestays, which will be attached later. Notice that the parts will be double-stitched, just like the original Air Force 1s. This will ensure a finished look.

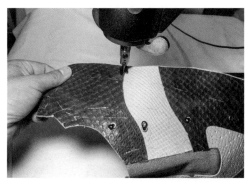

49 Use a patcher sewing machine to sew everything together in the same manner as with the core material and parts. Considering the fact that a used patcher sewing machine in good condition can fetch around $2,000, it is difficult to recommend buying one. However, it takes a really long time and much more concentration to complete this process by hand, so if you can get your hands on one, please take advantage of it.

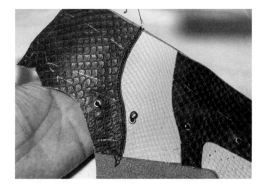

50 After stitching along the curves, a second line of stitching is applied just beside the first. The reason for the double stitching here is to ensure strength, but it is also to re-create the details of the Air Force 1. With a patcher sewing machine, the stitches are evenly spaced. This allows us to concentrate on getting the curved stitching right.

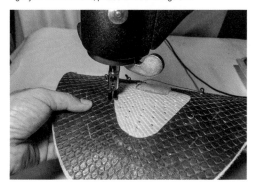

51 Let's double-stitch the toe box as well. When wearing your custom sneakers, the base of the toes is subjected to a lot of stress. If this area isn't strong enough, there is a high risk of the threads coming loose. Double-stitching by hand requires concentration, but the extra strength and look are worth the hassle.

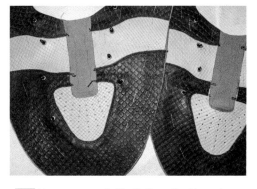

52 Here you can see double stitching on the side panels and toe box. You can see that the edge of the stitching is hanging over the area where the eyestays will be attached. After the double stitching is completed on both shoes, the Swoosh and eyestays can be attached. Finally, the details of the entire sneaker can now be seen.

CUSTOMIZATION SKILL 14

Installing Swoosh Parts
Position, Glue, and Then Stitch

The NIKE Swoosh is attached to the side panels after the stitching is complete. While the quarters and toe box are double-stitched to ensure strength, the Swoosh is attached with a single stitch after being glued in place. Needless to say, the single stitching for the Swoosh is also the same as the original Air Force 1.

53 When cutting out the part, be sure to check the position of the Swoosh by referring to the leather-marking pen line. After confirming the positioning, apply rubber cement to both sides of the adhesive surface and temporarily fix the Swoosh. If you want to fix the parts completely at this stage, sand the surface of the side panel and pressure-bond with sneaker glue.

54 The Swoosh is temporarily attached to the inside and outside side panels. The sneakers are finally starting to look like NIKES! There is no problem if you repeat the gluing and sewing process for each Swoosh individually, but for efficiency, it would be better to glue the four Swooshes on both sides first.

55 Single-stitch the Swoosh on. There are loops for the overlaces near the Swoosh, so be careful not to snag them when sewing. There are no rules about where to start sewing the Swoosh on, but start on the heel side for the best results.

56 Single-stitching along the edge of the Swoosh completes the side panel stitching. Here we used the same color thread as the base color, but if you want a more casual look, you can change the color of the thread. If you use yellow thread in this process, your custom sneakers will have a little extra pop.

>>

CUSTOMIZATION SKILL

Attach Eyestays

Cut Off Excess Core Material as You Install the Eyestays

After the laces are complete, the eyestays can be attached. The eyestays need to be strong, so it's important to be more careful than usual at this point. The eyelets will be punched after the lining is attached to the shoe. In this step, the eyestays are temporarily glued on the upper. Then, the edges are stitched and the excess core material is cut away.

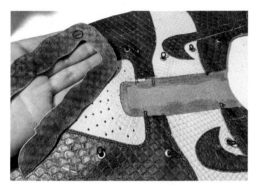

57 After confirming the position of the eyestays, apply rubber cement to the adhesive surface and temporarily fix in place. Since this part is in a conspicuous area, be sure to check everything carefully to avoid distortion. The snakeskin faux leather has relatively low levels of adhesion, but there is no need to worry, because the strength of the parts will be improved when they are stitched down to the upper.

58 Here the eyestays have been fixed temporarily. After confirming the position of the eyestays, cut off the excess core material left behind for the purpose of matching up shapes. Since this part has many curves, it is better to use leather scissors to cut the core material. However, the core material is also thick enough that it is easy to use too much force, so proceed with caution.

59 After cutting off the excess core material from the tongue area, stitch along the edge of the eyestays with a patcher sewing machine. The eyestays have a loose, wavy line that needs to be traced carefully. Patch sewing machines can easily change stitching direction, and the stitching is less affected by the depth of the machine itself. They are great for sewing large leather parts together.

60 Here the parts around the eyestays are sewn on. At this stage, the eyestay part of the shoe is sewn only to the side panel because the lining needs to be sewn to the shoe's tongue later. At this stage, the upper parts and core material are almost completely sewn, so you can now get an idea of the firm texture of the leather.

>>

Making the Tongue

CUSTOMIZATION SKILL

Create Leather Tongues That Add Elegance

For this example, instead of the nylon mesh shoe tongue that is often used in the original Air Force 1, a luxurious leather shoe tongue will be made. Also, instead of using a single piece of leather alone as the tongue, we will insert a cushioning material to improve the fit. There are surely many fans who feel that the cushioned shoe tongue has the "right look."

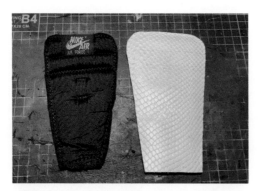

61 A pattern was made by referencing a dismantled Air Force 1 tongue. The surface parts were cut from the yellow leather used for the side panels. The customizer who worked on this project said, "A thinner leather than the one we are using is actually ideal in this case." If you are concerned about the thickness of the material, you may want to use a skiving knife to shave it down a bit.

62 Here's the front and back of the tongue along with some cushioning material. The cushioning material used here is a double layer of 10 mm / ¾" thick sponge purchased at a home improvement store. There is no rule on the thickness of the cushioning material, but if it is too thin or too soft, it will be difficult to get a good fit when wearing the shoe. That being said, adjust the thickness based around sneakers you usually wear.

63 The sponge is cut one size smaller than the leather. It is then sprayed with the appropriate "spray glue" and attached to the back of the leather. The glue doesn't need to be very strong, because the edges of the tongue will be sewn later. Actually, some glues are incompatible with sponges, so we need to check the properties of the adhesive before buying it

64 This photo shows the sponge sandwiched and glued between the two tongue parts. In this example, the material used for the back of the tongue is thin leather, about 1 mm / ¹⁄₁₆" thick. This material is also used for lining. After this, the edges of the parts will be temporarily fixed with double-sided tape, so make sure you have enough space for taping.

Making the Shoe Tongue

Leather Borders Add a Sense of Luxury

CUSTOMIZATION SKILL 17

The leather parts and sandwiched cushioning material are sewn together to create the tongue. If you use leather tape as trim around the edges, you will get a more luxurious look. However, the shoe tag—which is the "face" of the sneaker—and

the lace loop in the center of the tongue—which is often seen on old-school sneakers—need to be balanced with the rest of the design. We will examine these elements later.

65 Here the edges of the leather parts have been attached together with double-sided tape. The detail of the tongue should be almost the same as the one removed from the dismantled Air Force 1. Of course, if you want to create a different atmosphere from the original, you could try changing the tongue length.

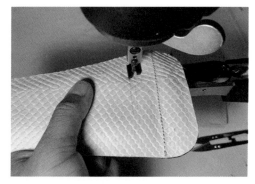

66 Use the details of the original as a reference, stitch across the tongue, and sew all the components together. If the stitching is slanted or distorted, it will stand out in a bad way once completed. Before you start sewing, it is essential to draw perfectly straight lines with a leather-marking pen and pay attention to avoid any distortion of the stitches.

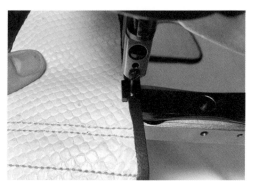

67 After the tongue has been stitched widthwise, we will sew leather binding strips to the edges. It's easier to temporarily fix the binding before sewing, but if the double-sided tape is sticking out from the edge, it will look pretty bad. It is better to use a relatively inconspicuous leather glue for temporary fixing.

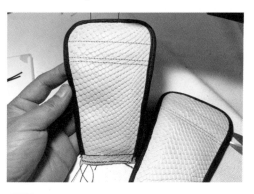

68 After sewing the binding to the edge of the tongue, our preparations are complete. The leather used for the binding is the same soft cowhide used for the backside of the tongue, about 1 mm / ¹⁄₁₆" thick. Recently, collaboration sneakers that have no sewing around the tongue, thus exposing the cushioning material, have been released. It would be interesting to try something like that someday.

>>

Cutting Out Lining
Making Lining Parts from Thin, Flexible Leather

Next, let's move on to the process of making the sneaker lining. Most sneaker linings are made from woven fabric, but here we cut our parts from highly flexible leather of about 1 mm / $\frac{1}{16}$" thick. The use of leather for the lining gives the sneakers a luxurious look, which goes well with our full upper customization using high-quality snakeskin faux leather.

69 The patterns for the toe area that are made by disassembling the lining removed from the Air Force 1. The details were copied onto 1 mm / $\frac{1}{16}$" thick leather with a leather-marking pen. The material used for the lining must have a certain amount of "foot slip," and if it is made of a material with poor "foot slip" such as suede, it will be difficult to get the shoe on.

70 The lining that goes from the center of the upper and around the heel is set up in the same manner as the toe portion. In this pattern, the center part corresponds to the heel. This is a very large part, so be careful not to shift the pattern when copying the details onto the material. By the way, the leather for the parts is the same as the material used for the back of the tongue.

71 Here, the quarter and vamp parts for the lining have been temporarily fixed. It is difficult to see in the image, but the lining around the collar is doubled to increase strength. The leather used for the lining needs to be flexible, but just because it is thin doesn't mean it is soft. Also, it should be noted that it is difficult to get a feel for the texture from a web store.

72 The lining is covering a last that is compatible with the Air Force 1. See how the detail looks like a slipper without soles? These types of lasts can be purchased from certain custom sneaker brands. It is a very important tool that is essential for fully enjoying upper customization.

Sewing the Lining and Heel Parts Together
Zigzag Stitching on the Heels for Durability

Continuing from the previous section, let's proceed to make the upper parts. We will check the balance between the lining and upper parts and sew them together at each sewing point. Since there is no "seam allowance" for the heel part, we will align the cross section of the parts and secure with cloth tape. A "zigzag stitch" will then be used to stitch the heel together. This stitching technique prevents the thread from unraveling when machine-sewing.

73 Check the balance of the lining parts and upper when they are wrapped around the last. When the customization is complete, the sneaker will be made of three layers of leather: the upper, the lining, and the core.

74 After confirming the balance, sew the toe and heel of the lining together with black thread that is the same color as the leather. When attaching to the upper, sew so that the edges of the lining are exposed. That way, if you need to dispose of any threads, you can dispose of them on the flesh side (backside) of the leather and just adjust so they won't be noticeable when finished.

75 Once the lining is in, it is time to sew the heel section of the upper. Unlike the other parts of the shoe, there is no seam allowance here. So, it is necessary to use a different technique to fix them together so that the edges are aligned. The customizer for this project used standard cloth tape and just attached it to the back of the upper.

76 The parts can now be sewn together with a "zigzag stitch," a stitch that moves back and forth along the joining edge. We will be adding reinforcing parts later, so it is important to first mark the width of the reinforcing parts on the heel with a leather-marking pen. Then, carefully apply zigzag stitches so they don't go beyond the designated width.

>>

Zigzag Stitching on the Heel

Remove as Much of the Securing Cloth Tape as Possible

The heel part of the upper needs to be sewn together with a zigzag stitch to finish this portion. Many ordinary home sewing machines have a "zigzag stitch" option. It should be noted here that it is quite difficult to sew uniform stitches on a patcher sewing machine because we have to change sewing directions frequently. Even though this area will be hidden in the end, it is always best for the customizer to finish such invisible parts well.

77 Here we see the heel section with the zigzag stitching completed. The width of the stitching isn't uniform. That's fine. The important thing is that the leather-marking pen lines on both sides of the stitching don't protrude. This line is the width of the reinforcing parts to be attached in the next process, and if the stitches are within the width of this line, the heel area can be beautifully finished in the style of Air Force 1.

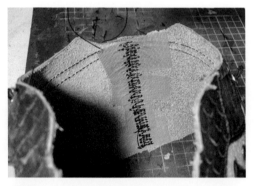

78 Zigzag stitching on the heel as seen from the inside. You can clearly see the zigzagging nature of this stitch on the inside of the shoe. It would be easier to see the zigzag stitching on the outside of the shoe if the thread was a different color from the base color. However, considering the risk of it jumping out at the viewer, it is wise to use a thread color that minimizes the "bling" in this area.

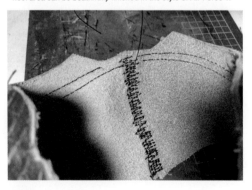

79 After checking the finish of the zigzag stitching, let's remove as much of the cloth tape that was used to secure the parts as possible. If the cloth tape isn't removed after completion, there is always the possibility that it will constantly irritate, or even stick to, the heel. Let's eliminate that risk.

80 The thread used by the customizer who worked on this project is called Ace Crown's polyester 8 oz. thread. It is readily available at online stores and comes in over 300 colors. If you want to check out the subtle differences in coloration between their threads, you can get the Ace Crown's color sample book.

Sew Heel Reinforcement Parts
Not Just for Reinforcement but Also as an Accent

A colorful reinforcement part is added to cover the zigzag stitching on the heel. This accent isn't found on the Air Jordan 1 or Dunk, but it definitely adds to the uniqueness of our customization. We will use yellow snakeskin faux leather, rather than navy, in order to really grab people's attention. The parts are attached with rubber glue and stitched with a patcher sewing machine, just like the other parts we have been working with.

81 Cut out the parts from the disassembled Air Force 1 and attach them to the heel where the two pieces are sewn together. If you use the same color as the base, you can get a more relaxed look, but to add character we used the same bright-yellow leather as we used on the side panel and tongue.

82 Apply rubber cement to the backside of the reinforcing parts and temporarily fix them in place, using the marked lines as a guide. For small parts like these, it is difficult to apply glue with a large spatula. I recommend getting a small spatula from a dollar store, or you could even use a "wooden spatula" made from an ice cream stick.

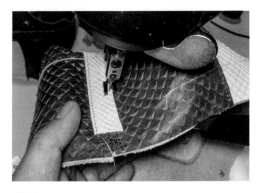

83 Use yellow thread to sew on the reinforcing parts. Be sure to stitch both the long side and the short side. You want to keep this stitching as straight and precise as possible to produce a really clean look. If you are not confident about sewing straight lines, you can use a leather-marking pen to draw guidelines in advance for better accuracy.

84 Here we have the heel joint with reinforcement parts. You can see that the zigzag stitching that was done earlier is completely covered. The upper and lower edges will be hidden by other parts in subsequent processes. This process doesn't require strength, but if you want to use a knot, you should tie it where it will be hidden.

>>

CUSTOMIZATION SKILL

Attaching the Backstay
Add Strength By Inserting Core Material

After covering the zigzag stitching, the "backstay" is attached to the mouth on the heel side of the shoe. When explaining sneaker details, the parts that make up the heel area are often referred to as "heel counter parts," but the correct name for these parts is "backstay." The backstay is the part that is grasped—or pressed against when using a shoehorn—when pulling on the sneaker. It must be strong enough to withstand serious wear. The best way to add strength is by inserting a core material.

85 Cut out core material for the backstay from the split leather. Use the original part as a reference. Since it would be too thick if we applied core material to the entire part, we designed the core material to be attached only to the upper edge of the backstay. At this point, the lines drawn on the parts can be copied onto masking tape and pasted onto the split leather as a substitute for a pattern.

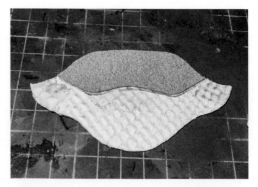

86 The cutout core material is temporarily fixed to the backstay with leather adhesive. The center of the core material is designed to be a little short because it interferes with the reinforcement parts attached to the zigzag stitching. After temporarily attaching the piece in the expected place, apply adhesive to the entire surface of the area visible in the photo. Then, attach it to the upper part of the heel section of the shoe.

87 After the backstay is temporarily fixed, sew it along the bottom edge with yellow thread. The fabric of the part that overlaps the Swoosh and heel reinforcement parts is thick, so it would take a lot of effort to sew by hand. It's not necessary to sew the top of this part at this stage, because the lining still needs to be sewn.

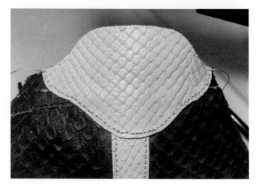

88 Here are the upper parts with the backstay attached. We chose yellow leather for the backstay, which is also used for the other parts, but if you want to give the Air Force 1 an old-school look, a white backstay is a pretty good choice. In that case, the thread should also be white as well, so that the stitches don't stand out too much.

>>

Sewing the Lining

CUSTOMIZATION SKILL

Sewing the Upper and Lining Together along the Collar

After modeling the upper parts around the heel, let's attach the leather lining parts. The leather lining parts selected for this project give the sneakers an overwhelmingly luxurious feel compared to ordinary sneakers. It's a detail worth spending a lot of time on. Note that we will be sewing only around the collar of the shoes right now, since we will be attaching the reinforcement parts and cushioning material later on.

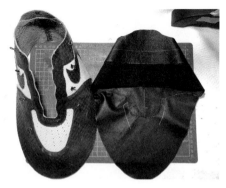

89 Here are the upper parts and lining. At this point, the upper and lining have a strong "cut out of leather" look. However, when the upper and lining are sewn together and the reinforced parts and cushioning materials are attached in between them, the overall volume will increase, and the sneaker-like details will magically appear.

90 Lay the lining over the upper so that everything is aligned. After sewing them together, the lining is flipped inside out so that the grain side is exposed on the inside of the sneaker. Technically, it is possible to expose the flesh side of the lining to the wearer, but it would cause too much friction between the lining and the sock and make it hard to put on and remove the sneaker.

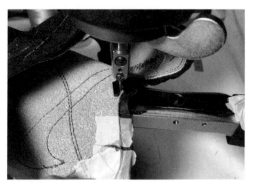

91 Sew on the lining that will become the collar of the sneakers. Before you start sewing, don't forget to fix the parts in the correct position with masking tape to prevent shifting. Once you sew up to the first taped position, stop, remove a little of the masking tape, and then continue and repeat the process.

92 After you complete the stitching, flip the lining into the inside of the upper. You can see that the lining covers the edges of the upper part, giving it a sneaker-like detail. This is the final stage of creating the uppers, where the customizer's sense of style is reflected.

>>

Create Core Material to Reinforce the Heel

Use Leather Skiver to Adjust Thickness of Core Material

CUSTOMIZATION SKILL 24

Making the core material for the heel is an important process that ensures not only the strength of the shoe, but also the stability of the heel. In many cases, when making leather shoes by hand, parts cut from split leather are soaked in cement and later dried to make the core material harder. However, in this case, a core material that has both strength and flexibility is created using double-laminated split leather.

93 Using the shape of the core material taken from the Air Force 1 as a reference, the parts are cut out. In this example, the perimeter of the parts—made of two pieces of leather—were trimmed to be thinner than the original with a leather skiver. Another point here is to cut a V shape in the center of the parts so that they will maintain a natural curve when installed.

94 Next, use a leather skiver to adjust the thickness of both ends of the core material. At this point the core is made of two pieces of split leather that have been pasted together. The lower edge of the part is cut in a gently sloped V shape. The leather skiver we used can be found on the internet for around $10. Leather thickness is adjusted by using the blade in the gap at the tip.

95 Compare the thickness of the original and the two pieces of split leather pasted together. The core material for the heel made here is larger than the original part, and the lower line of the part is designed to bite into the midsole. The thickness needs to be adjusted again with the skiver to avoid unnecessary bumps where the upper joins the sole.

96 Apply rubber cement to both the upper and the core material and glue together. It is important to attach the parts at a point that doesn't interfere with the stitching line. It will be difficult to proceed if the parts protrude down to where the upper and midsole are sewn together. At this point, it is a good idea to draw a guideline for the attachment position, all the while referring to the pattern made at the beginning of this customization.

>>

Cushion Material Installation
Changing the Thickness of the Sponge Will Change the Size

After attaching the core material to the heel section, let's move on to the process of attaching the cushioning material. The cushioning material used here is made from commercially available sponge sheets. We will refer to the heel section of the pattern we made for the lining, and paste on multiple layers of sponge to adjust the thickness. I would love to tell you exactly what thickness to use, but it varies depending on the hardness of the sponge sheets. In the end you just have to refer to the sneakers at hand and adjust the thickness to your liking.

97 The thickness of the cushioning material cut out from the sponge sheet is adjusted by laminating thin sponge sheets on top of each other. The thicker the cushioning material, the better the hold, but the tighter the shoe will fit. On the other hand, if the cushioning material is too thin, the shoe will be loose, and you'll need to tighten the laces excessively.

98 Use rubber cement to attach the cushioning material so that its center and the centerline of the heel part are aligned. To be honest, it is difficult to use a really thick sponge sheet because it needs to be bent a lot during the following process. If possible, it is better to use a sponge sheet with a thickness of around 1 cm / ⅜" and adjust to fit.

99 After confirming that the cushioning material is set, let's reset the lining. The volume of the cushioning is a unique detail of the sneaker. It isn't found in most leather shoes. The cushioning material will be attached in a later process called "lasting," so there is no need to glue it firmly at this stage.

100 Next, the lining and the parts around the eyestays are sewn together. Unlike with the collar, the lining and upper parts are sewn together with double stitches. Cut off the lining where it sticks out below the eyestays with leather craft scissors after stitching is complete.

>>

CUSTOMIZATION
SKILL

Finishing around the Tongue
Eyelet Finishing and Tongue Installation

The finishing construction touches on the upper are the eyelets and tongue attachment. The Air Force 1, originally released in 1982, has more eyelets than modern basketball shoes, a detail that gives it an old-school look. Here, the eyelets are punched using the pattern cut out previously. Then, the upper and the tongue are sewn appropriately.

101 Copy the positions of the eyelets from the pattern onto the parts. Since the Air Force 1 is characterized by its wave-shaped eyestays, it is best to keep the wave-shaped layout in mind as you work to create a custom sneaker with a distinct Air Force 1 look.

102 A rotary leather punch is used to make the eyelets. This tool works well for eyelet punching and makes for a stress-free situation. In this example, eyelet holes are 3.5 mm / ⅛" in diameter. They are almost the same as the original. If you don't have a rotary leather punch, you can use a hole punch with a similar diameter.

103 The eyelets have been punched and the eyestays are in place. You can see how the eyelets are subtly offset while still remaining perpendicular to each other. The eyelets for the overlaces were metal, but in this case we are just using drilled holes to maintain that old-school look.

104 Once the eyestays are in place, it is time to sew the tongue onto the upper. You can also attach the shoe label and lace loops at this stage, but it is easier to get the balance right if you do it after the entire production process is complete.

>>

Preparing to Last the Sneakers
Moving from Making to Lasting

The making of the uppers is complete. From here, we proceeded to the "lasting" process, which is the highlight of all upper customization. Lasting is the process of putting the upper parts on a wooden shoe last, pulling the leather with special pliers

called "lasting pliers," and then fixing the leather with nails so that it conforms to the details of the shoe last. Unlike leather shoes, here the sole unit is taken from other sneakers, but the process requires skills comparable to those of a shoemaker.

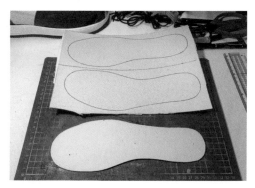

105 We will prepare the insole to hold the upper in place during the lasting process. In some cases, "insole leather" with a thickness of around 5 mm / ¼" is used, but in this case, pulp board soaked with synthetic rubber or natural rubber is used because the thickness of the insole may be insufficient for bonding the sole unit.

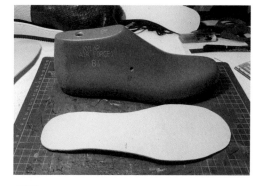

106 Prepare the shoe last that will form the shape of the upper when lasting. Here, we prepared a shoe last compatible with a size 11 Air Force 1. This last is made with details that correspond to the design and size of the sneaker. That being said, it really can't be used for anything other than a size 11 Air Force 1.

107 In the lasting process, the upper, stretched with lasting pliers, is fixed to the insole with nails. There are no special nails here; just choose nails that are easy to use. In general, however, "roundheaded nails" around 19 mm / ¾" in length seem to be the most popular. Lasting is a job that requires a lot of nails, so be sure to pick up more than you need.

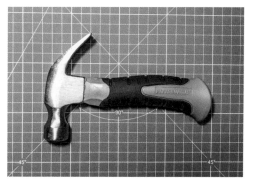

108 When nails are used, hammers are naturally needed. Shoemakers use two types of hammers, one for the uppers and one for the soles. Customizers often use hammers with a rubber grip (as seen here), but in reality you can use any hammer you are comfortable with.

>>

Attaching Insoles to Shoe Lasts

CUSTOMIZATION SKILL

Lasting Involves Fixing Parts by Bending the Hammered-In Nails

Attaching the insoles to the last using nails. The insoles used here are made from "Bontex," a cellulose material used in leather crafting. Bontex can be purchased at leathercraft stores. The 1.3 mm / 1/16" thickness, "extra thick" kind, is suitable for the insoles of our shoes. Even though it is labeled as extra thick, it is much thinner than the cowhide insole board and is thus easier to cut out with leather scissors.

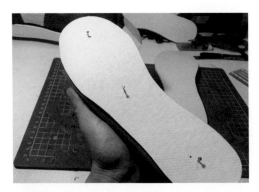

109 After aligning everything with the last, roundheaded nails in the front, center, and back of the insole board. It goes without saying that if everything isn't properly aligned, the finished product will be distorted. When hammering in the nails, don't hammer them all the way into the wood mold. Leave about 1/3 of the 19 mm / 3/4" nail above the insole.

110 Leave about 1/3 of the nails sticking out and then roll them over using a hammer. The purpose of this is to "keep" the insole board from being lifted by the impact of the following processes. Also, it is easier to remove the nails, since they need to be removed after the lasting is complete. There is no rule on the direction in which the nails should be hammered down; it only necessary to change the direction of the nails to prevent the bottom from shifting.

111 After the insole is attached to the last, the upper is placed over the top of the last. If the laces are loose at this point, the area around the tongue will be unnaturally wide when finished. In order not to waste any of the work done up to this point, it is important to tightly tie the shoelaces on the upper before wrapping it around the last.

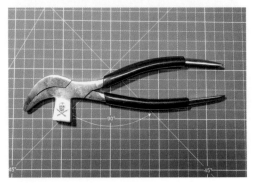

112 Lasting pliers are a specialized tool for stretching leather on an upper. Japanese shoemakers call them "alligators" because they have a silhouette that resembles the mouth of an alligator. The "alligators" shown here are sold by the world's leading custom sneaker brand, "The Shoe Surgeon."

>>

Temporary Lasting of the Upper
How to Perform the First Steps for Temporary Lasting

The upper is pulled strongly toward the sole with lasting pliers. When the leather is sufficiently stretched, you can nail it to the sole. There are two steps to the lasting process. First, tentative lasting is done to "acclimate" the upper to the shoe last. If there are no problems, the lasting is done by attaching reinforcing parts to the toe. In this section, we will introduce the tentative lasting process.

113 When checking fit, the upper and lining leathers are both grasped by the lasting pliers at the same time and firmly stretched toward the sole. This process isn't done just once. It is repeated in slightly different positions over and over, and once the leather has been stretched sufficiently, nails are driven into the last to fix in place.

114 The heel side is similarly stretched by sandwiching the upper and lining leather between the pliers. It may seem uncomfortable to hammer nails into the carefully worked upper parts, but the sections where the nails are hammered in will be hidden once the sole unit is attached. So, don't worry about the nail marks, and just be sure to nail the stretched leather firmly.

115 Here, the entire upper has been temporarily lasted. All the nails that were hammered in are pulled out when proceeding to the main lasting process, so there is no need to use a hammer to lay them down at this point. The only thing to check here is whether the leather upper fits the shoe last. If any parts are loose, just use the lasting pliers again to stretch the leather tight.

116 After making sure that the leather that makes up the upper is sufficiently stretched around the last, remove the nails from the toe and roll the parts back. After that, stretch the lining with lasting pliers again and nail to the shoe last. This is all preparation for attaching the toe reinforcement pieces between the lining and the upper.

>>

Lasting the Toe Section
Cut Off Excess Lining and Work the Adhesive Surface Flat

Once the toe lining is lasted, we will glue it to the insole board. The reason for working on the toe part first is that we need to attach the reinforcement parts between the lining and the upper before the main lasting is performed. After attaching the lining to the insole, we will cut off the excess leather from the lasting process to make it easier to proceed with the main lasting.

117 After confirming that the lining is snug, one of the nails can be pulled out with lasting pliers or a nail punch. The gap created is then glued in place with adhesive. Pulling out multiple nails in this process increases the risk of "sagging" or distortion of the stretched lining, so it is best to avoid temptation. This process requires a lot of steady work.

118 The adhesive used here must be very strong. The customizer this time was using "Non-Toluene No-Tape 9820NT" (Barge and Master Brand substitutes can be used). No-Tape 9820NT is mixed with a hardener, so it takes time and effort to use frequently. But it hardens faster than ordinary adhesives, and its transparent finish makes it suitable for lasting.

119 Once the glue has been applied to the area where the nail was removed, the leather is stretched with lasting pliers and nailed back into place. It requires a lot of concentration to repeat this routine over and over. Needless to say, this is a process that will improve the finish of your custom sneakers, and it is therefore well worth the effort.

120 Inevitably, there will be some excess leather during the lasting process. In the case of an All Upper customization, the upper itself will be laminated to the sole unit. Excess leather should be trimmed off to ensure a flat surface for smooth bonding.

CUSTOMIZATION SKILL

Lasting the Heel and Prepping Reinforcement Material
Use Special Core Material Specifically for Toe Caps

While waiting for the toe lining glue to dry, we can proceed to the second half of the process, the main lasting of the heel and quarter areas. The basic process is the same as the temporary lasting, the difference being that adhesive is applied to both sides of the insole board and lining, as well as to the adhesive surface of the upper. Then, everything is firmly attached with nails. Once the heel and quarter section of the shoe are lasted, cut off the excess leather and start preparing the reinforcement parts.

121 After removing the nails from the heel and quarter section of the shoe and applying adhesive to the upper, lining, and insole, the leather is again pulled with lasting pliers. Stretch well and hammer in place. This time, not all the nails are hammered back into the last. Some are bent over so that they face inward, and then they are hammered flat as shown.

122 You can use scissors or cutters to cut off the excess leather, but you can also use a safety beveler to great effect, although it should be noted that this technique requires a bit of skill. The leather safety beveler shown in the photo has a blade in the hole at the tip. You can insert the excess leather into the hole and then just trim it off. These bevelers are highly regarded for their sharpness, even with thick leather, and can be purchased online.

123 The toe box lining has now been beautifully applied. It is nice and taut and fits the last perfectly. After attaching the reinforcing parts to the toe area, the upper is covered again, and the lasting process is complete. Lasting tends to scare people away from leather work because it sounds like a very specialized skill. But with the proper preparation, it can be enjoyed by anyone.

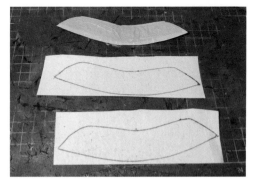

124 The toe reinforcement material used in this project is called "Polytex 066." Substitute materials, like Celastic, can be found online. I put masking tape on the toe part and traced the shape to make a pattern. Use this pattern to copy the details onto Polytex (or something similar) and cut out the reinforcement parts for both feet.

Toe Core Installation and Main Lasting
Curve Toe Core Using Solvent and Attach to the Last

Air Force 1 with full upper customization and toe cores installed. Toe cores are reinforcement materials attached between the upper and lining of the toe. In this case, Polytex 066 (Celastic is a suitable substitute), which is sold specifically as a toe reinforcement material, is used to increase strength of the toe area.

125 I cut pieces for the toe cores from a sheet of "Polytex 066" and applied them to the toe portion of the lining. Polytex 066 is pretty stiff, so, even though the lower edge lines up with the sole, the upper edge of the part doesn't correspond to the curve of the lining. The overlap is repaired by utilizing the characteristics of the material itself.

126 The Polytex used here is a sheet about 1 mm / $^{1}/_{16}$" thick. It can be purchased cheaply and comes in sheets of 48 cm × 70 cm / 18$^{7}/_{8}$" × 27 ½". It is not a material that is familiar to most people, but it is also used for toe cores in custom leather shoes. Somewhat surprisingly, this type of core material temporarily softens in certain solvents. The solvent used here is Diabond's "Sheet Dip," but acetone or methyl ethyl ketone can be substituted.

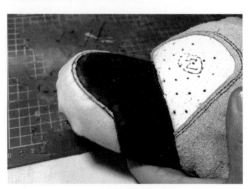

127 Once the Polytex is softened with solvent, form it to the toe cap. The solvent-soaked Polytex will not stay soft forever. It will harden over time. It's essential to do the main lasting of the toe area while the Polytex is still soft, in order to force it to conform to the curve of the toe cap.

128 After attaching the toe cores, the upper parts are immediately placed over the toes and lasted with pliers. For the best toe strength, it is better to glue the upper to the lining. But if the lining is well lasted, it won't shift when worn anyway. After all this work is complete, let's move on to finishing the sole.

>>

CUSTOMIZATION SKILL

Lasting the Toe Section
Try to Keep the Glued-Down Sole as Flat as Possible

After securely attaching the center of the parts and doing the main lasting, cut excess leather to make the sole as flat as possible. For this All Upper customization, we assume that you will be attaching a dismantled Air Force 1 sole unit or a sole from another sneaker. If there are any differences between the glue on the sole side and the upper, not only will stability be reduced, but in the worst-case scenario, comfort will suffer greatly.

129 Now, while attaching the upper to the insole boards with the appropriate glues, it is necessary to cut off any leather that was left over from the lasting process. The basic technique here is the same as that used when lasting: apply adhesive to the part where the nail was removed, last again, and then cut off the excess leather with a beveler.

130 Here, the upper parts have been attached to the insole board, and the excess leather has been removed. After hammering in about ⅔ of the nails to secure the leather, use a hammer to bend them down toward the center of the shoe. Although there is no definite rule on the number of nails you need to use, a good number will be needed if the shoe is to fit snugly around the shoe last.

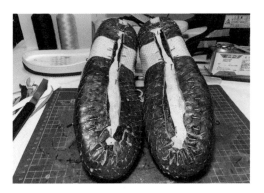

131 Both shoes are now lasted. The glued surfaces of the soles are now flat as well, so they can be attached without any problems. In addition to the nails that hold the uppers in place, all the nails that were used to attach the soles to the lasts are removed in the later process. So, be careful not to hide the nails during lasting.

132 Lasting is now complete. They have such a beautiful silhouette. It is very reminiscent of the Air Force 1. Custom shoe lasting is one of the criteria that best show off the skill of the customizer. "LASTING" may seem like quite the hurdle, but if you have a last, the correct tools, and a good amount of concentration, it is not an impossible hurdle to clear.

>>

Preparing the Sole Unit for Installation
Boiling Air Force 1s to Soften the Glue Used to Attach the Soles

Once the upper is ready, the sole unit is prepared for installation. The Air Force 1 that we are going to remove the sole from is a collaboration model with Magic Stick, commonly known as the "High VIP." I can hear sneaker fans shouting, "What a waste!"

However, the white-and-black color of the sole goes exceptionally well with our upper, so it has to be sacrificed in order to produce our desired look.

133 To balance the color with the upper, the customizer chose to take the sole from a collaboration model nicknamed the "High VIP," released in December 2018. The product is inspired by a nightclub. The ankle strap, which looks very much like a nightclub wristband, gave rise to the nickname.

134 The Air Force 1 uses a sole application method called "Opanka." The sole is glued on first and then sewn on. To remove the sole from our donor shoe, the stitching that connects the sole to the upper is first removed. It is best to use a ripper, which can be purchased at a handicraft store, since it makes this process comparatively easy.

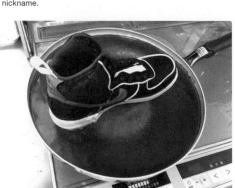

135 The adhesive used for attaching sneaker soles softens and becomes easier to remove when heated. In this case, we chose the bold method of boiling the sneakers in a frying pan partially filled with hot water. It is a bold approach, but it is also widely known that boiling sneakers is very effective for removing soles. As a matter of fact, this method is commonly seen on various social media sites.

136 After removing the sole unit, you can see that the airbag, the origin of the term Air in Air Force 1, is embedded in the sole. New sneakers tend to still be strongly adhered. If the adhesive is too stubborn, you can try using a syringe to dribble acetone on the adhesive surface. This will help dissolve the glue and make the sole easier to remove.

>>

Sole Adhesion Pretreatment
Sand Surface to Increase Glue Adhesion

Even though it appears as though the Air Force 1 sole is stitched directly to the upper, in reality the parts are just glued together and then stitched for reinforcement. In order to make an All Upper custom Air Force 1, the sole must first be glued and then sewn. To ensure high strength, it is important to choose the right sneaker adhesive and to pretreat the material to get better adhesion.

137 Once the lasted upper parts are secured, use lasting pliers or a hammer to remove the nails from the shoe last. Don't forget to remove the three nails that hold the insole to the last, and not just the the nails that hold the leather parts together. In order to make this job easier, you can always leave some of the nails bent rather than driving them all the way in.

138 Once all the nails have been pulled, the glued surfaces of the upper parts are sanded with coarse sandpaper to make the glue in the next step stick better. For Air Force 1s, you need to draw a line where the edge of the sole and the upper will be, and sand all the way to that edge. The reason for this is that these shoes need a little extra adhesive strength where the sole turns up.

139 Remove as much of the old adhesive as possible from the sole unit. The edges are especially prone to glue residue. Carefully remove with a Dremel or similar tool, taking care not to damage the sole. If there are lumps of glue still on the edges, use a cotton swab and acetone to rub it off.

140 Here are the cleaned surfaces of both the upper and sole. We used snakeskin faux leather for the upper material, and it should be noted that this type of leather is not very strong. So, we have to be really careful when polishing to remove the scaly details. After the pretreatment, it is time to attach the sole.

>>

CUSTOMIZATION SKILL

Apply Sneaker Glue to the Bonding Surface
Barge Cement Is the Standard When Gluing on Sneaker Soles

After the pretreatment, it was time to attach the sole to the upper parts. The adhesive used here is Barge Cement, a special adhesive for sneakers that is also known for being exceptionally good when performing a "sole swap." Barge Cement is trusted by customizers around the world for its ease of use and high adhesive strength.

141 The Barge Cement used in this process is called "Super Stik." It has enhanced adhesive strength. As with the relatively easy-to-find Barge "Infinity," a simple brush is attached to the lid of the can. This makes it easy to apply without the need for a separate brush. However, the brush on the lid of the can isn't very easy to work with, so you may want to buy your own brush from a dollar store.

142 The entire surface, up to the line, has been coated with Barge Cement. Barge Cement doesn't require a primer. It is allowed to dry until it doesn't stick to the fingers anymore before pressure bonding. You don't need to rush to work with this adhesive like you do with general glues. Just make sure you apply it without leaving any remnants.

143 Barge Cement has been applied to the upper and the sole. The drying time varies depending on temperature and humidity, but as a rule of thumb, it should take about an hour. In the end, touch the glued surface with your finger to make sure it doesn't stick. Use the drying time to apply Barge Cement to the other shoe.

144 After making sure the glue is dry, heat the surface with a heat gun. Barge Cement needs to be heated before gluing. However, there are other types of sneaker adhesives, such as those that require a primer, that don't need to be heated before gluing. Be sure to check the manufacturer's recommendations before use.

>>

07 CUSTOMIZATION SKILL

Bonding the Upper and Sole
Bond Carefully So That the Soles Will Not Shift

After applying heat to the dried adhesive with a heat gun, the upper and sole are pasted together. You can now attach the two surfaces together like applying a sticker. If misaligned, use a heat gun to peel the sole off again, then use acetone to remove the glue and reattach using the same process. Reattaching the soles requires a fair amount of effort, so try to put everything together correctly first.

145 The customizer who worked on this project started gluing from the toe part of the shoe. There is no specific way to apply the sole to the upper. If you want to start gluing from the heel side, go ahead. Just choose the method that is easiest for you.

146 If you spend a lot of time positioning the sole exactly where you want before you start gluing, it can be helpful to apply heat to the adhesive again. As mentioned in the previous section, many sneaker adhesives are designed to be applied and dried before being glued together. There is no need to rush this process. The shortcut to success is to be careful with the task the first time around.

147 After the upper and sole are bonded, apply weight to the adhesive surface and pressure-bond firmly. Use a hammer to carefully pressure-bond the midsole, especially where it rolls up on the sides. That is where strength is really required. DON'T hit the sole with the hammer. Just apply pressure as if you are pressing against something soft.

148 The sole is now bonded. If the special glue is used correctly, it will be strong in this state. However, if we want to show our respect to details born in 1982, it is essential to reproduce the "Opanka method" of attaching the sole with thread. In the next step, we will apply the "Opanka method" to give the custom Air Force 1s their iconic look.

>>

Removing Uppers from the Shoe Last
There's Actually a Specific Tool for Removing the Last

Before employing the "Opanka method," the mold used for lasting is pulled out of the shoe. After the last is removed, it is best if the lining is taut. Once the last is removed, the "Opanka method" can finally be applied. Once the retro-style stitching is applied to the sole, the All Upper customization process, which started all the way back at cutting parts out of leather, is almost complete.

149 The screw hole in the upper part of the last is pushed onto a pin on a "Lasting Jack." The lasting process itself really tightens the leather around the shoe last, so it is quite hard to remove without using a tool like this.

150 You can use your body weight to "crack" the last and slide it out of the upper. There are many types of shoe lasts that don't articulate along their center. However, the ones that do are much easier to remove. It should be noted that there are only a few types of shoe lasts that are compatible with sneakers. It is not always easy to choose the right one for you, but if you ask around, you will find one that works.

151 The last has now been removed and we can see the insole board with its nail holes. After the Opanka process has been applied, insoles from a donor pair of Air Force 1s can be put in. However, we actually recommend using cork insoles for a more crafted look. For more cushioning, you can also use functional insoles or orthotics available at sports stores and shoe stores.

152 The Opanka method uses a hand-sewing tool for thick fabric and leather, called a "sewing awl," and special, twisted thread. The customizer who worked on this project used thread with a count of 00. The smaller the number, the thicker the thread, with 00 being the thickest.

>>

Attaching Soles Using the Opanka Method

CUSTOMIZATION SKILL

Recreate Sneaker Factory Processes by Hand Sewing

The sole is sewn to the upper by using the Opanka method. The Okanka method, which uses a sewing awl specifically made for leather and thick fabric, exposes the seams on the sole on purpose. Sneaker factories use special sewing machines to

do the work, but we can use a hand awl. This is a skill that is useful not just for customizing sneakers but also for repairing them, including sole swaps.

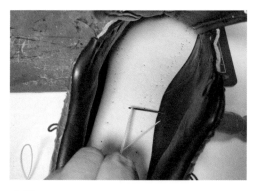

153 Insert the awl, already threaded, from the sole side straight into the interior of the shoe. Once the tip penetrates the inside of the shoe, pull loose end of the thread through to the interior of the shoe and leave it hanging inside the shoe. Next, insert the needle into the next hole along the stitching line, and pull the stitcher back slightly to make a small loop in the thread (as seen in the photo).

154 Next, thread the loose end of the thread (the one hanging inside the shoe) through the loop. After the thread has passed through the loop, pull on both ends with equal force to tighten the stitch. This process is repeated over and over all the way around the sole to sew it to the shoe. Be very careful not to stab yourself in the finger when working around the toe of the shoe. There isn't as much room!

155 Also note that stitching is performed by using the holes that are already in the sole. Actually, it isn't a big deal if you don't use the original holes, but it takes a lot of effort to push the needle through both the midsole rubber and the leather on the upper. Also, it is much easier to maintain the proper stitch spacing by using the holes left in the sole as a guideline.

156 Once you have finished stitching the entire sole, pull the thread out of the awl inside the shoe and tie it off inside to secure it. If the edge of the thread bothers you, you can use masking tape to attach it to the inside sole. It may be difficult to understand just from the text, but if you give it a try, you will find that it is easier to understand by actually moving your hands.

>>

Finishing the Tongue
Create Custom Tongues with Laser Engraving

Our All Upper custom is almost finished! The final touch is the tongue. The shoe tag is a detail that should be given a lot of attention, since it really stands out on the sneaker. To respect the original, a shoe tag from a donor pair of Air Force 1s can be transplanted onto the tongue. Here, though, an original logo has been laser-engraved onto leather material to create a unique tag. This adds to the sense of craftsmanship in this custom build.

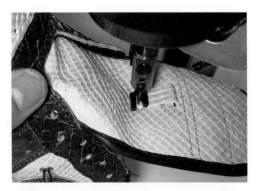

157 Before making our original shoe tag, let's attach the loop for the laces. Here, a long, thin piece of the yellow leather we used for the tongue has been used for the lace loop. It is sewn on with a patcher sewing machine. Be sure to carefully refer to the position of the lace loop on an original pair of Air Force 1s.

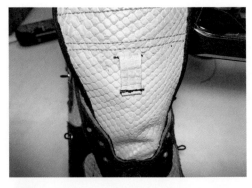

158 Even though many NIKE sneakers have lace loops that are simply cut into the shoe's tongue, we have sewn the lace loops onto the tongue so that they will be easier to use. You can choose whichever loop style you prefer.

159 After attaching the loops, it is time to make our original shoe tongue tag. To engrave the logo on the leather material, we will use a laser-engraving machine for home use. In the past, laser-engraving machines were very expensive, but in recent years they have become available for around $100. The one used by the customizer here is a midrange unit that can be purchased for around $200.

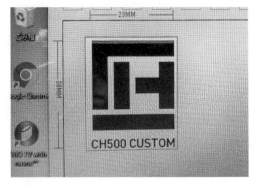

160 Install the provided drivers and software on your PC and then adjust the design and size of the logo as desired. The size of the actual engraved logo will be displayed on the PC screen, so check it carefully to make sure the balance is correct for your sneakers. By the way, this laser engraver can engrave on wood as well as leather.

NIKE AIR FORCE 1 LOW

Attaching the Original Shoe Tag
Highly Crafted All-Upper Customs Are Complete

Once the logo design is programmed into the engraver, the leather parts are cut into long, thin strips and engraved. As affordable engravers become more available, the number of people who use laser-engraving machines is rapidly increasing, especially DIY enthusiasts. In addition to the shoe tags shown here, it is also easy to make key chains, etc. with your engraver. With more experience you can even engrave directly on the sneaker itself.

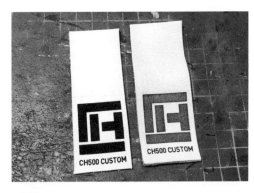

161 The leather parts for the tongue tag are placed in the laser-engraving machine, and the original logo is engraved. The transparent green plate seen in the image is a shield to prevent the laser beam from damaging your eyes. The engraving machine used here is compact, about 20 cm / 7⅞" square. However, the laser is sufficiently powerful to complete the engraving in a short amount of time.

162 The power of this engraver is adjustable. The higher the power, the more time it takes to engrave the logo. On the other hand, if set to a lower level, a light engraving can be done relatively quickly. Both logos are sharp, but for the shoe tag, we chose the light engraving to really let the texture of the leather pop.

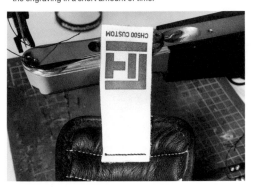

163 Sew on the engraved shoe tag. This time we will use a tag that goes up around to the back of the tongue. First, sew the tag on the backside in a straight line, using a patcher sewing machine. The sewing thread used in this process will be hidden by the parts on the front side of the shoe, so there is no need to be particular about the color.

164 The tag can now be wrapped over the top of the tongue and sewn onto the front of the tongue. Just to keep things clean, the ends of the thread are singed with a lighter. This also prevents them from unraveling. After this, thread both the regular laces and overlaces onto the upper and enjoy your fantastic workmanship.

>>

Complete

CUSTOMIZATION SKILL

Eye-Catching Overlaces

This Amazing Custom Pair of Sneakers Will Provide a Real Sense of Accomplishment

The All Upper customization process, described over more than forty pages, is now complete. Despite using the old-school yellow-and-navy-dyed Air Force 1 as a design base, the combination of luxurious leather and catchy overlaces strongly emphasizes the fact that this pair of sneakers is really special and one of a kind. We think that it is amazing that they are really artistic and yet practical to wear. It is true that customizing All Uppers requires some professional equipment, such as a patcher sewing machine and shoe lasts, as well as a certain amount of skill and craftsmanship to finish the job. However, if you are reading this book, you surely have these qualities in you! So, give it a shot! The All Upper is truly worth trying, since it gives you a sense of accomplishment like nothing else ever will!

CUSTOMIZER INFORMATION

@ch500usmade

With the motto of "Making sneakers you can't buy from a manufacturer," this customizer enjoys customization as a hobby and shows his work on Instagram and at custom sneaker events. His work has been praised as "More than a personal hobby" by many, but he has no plans to sell his sneakers at the moment.

Instagram@ch500usmade

CH500 CUSTOM

NIKE AIR FORCE 1 LOW

CH500 CUSTOM

Truly Custom Sneakers:
Works of Art That Are beyond Compare

ALL-UPPER CUSTOMIZATION
NIKE AIR FORCE 1 LOW & AIR JORDAN 1 HIGH

All Upper Customs
Every Skill Is Put to Practical Use

Once you have mastered the All Upper customization skills described here, you can apply them to many old-school sneakers. Although there are some hurdles to overcome when it comes to obtaining a compatible shoe last, once you have one, you can try your hand at making All Upper customs featuring the Air Jordan 1!

About the Author

The Customize Kicks Magazine team, led by its chief editor Yuji Sato, compiled this guide. Sato has been at the forefront of the Japanese sneaker culture for more than two decades. His experience includes founding the vintage sneaker store Hand Carry in Hiratsuka City and editing the mook *Sneaker Fanbook*.

Other Schiffer Books on Related Subjects:

How to Render Attractive Characters with COPIC Markers, Yasaiko Midorihana, ISBN 978-0-7643-6420-4

From the Platform: Subway Graffiti, 1983–1989, Paul Cavalieri, ISBN 978-0-7643-3723-9

The NES Omnibus: The Nintendo Entertainment System and Its Games, Brett Weiss: Vol. 1 (A–L), ISBN 978-0-7643-6068-8; Vol. 2 (M–Z), ISBN 978-0-7643-6248-4

ISBN: 978-0-7643-6553-9

Printed in China

Published by Schiffer Publishing, Ltd.
4880 Lower Valley Road
Atglen, PA 19310
Phone: (610) 593-1777; Fax: (610) 593-2002
Email: Info@schifferbooks.com
Web: www.schifferbooks.com

For our complete selection of fine books on this and related subjects, please visit our website at www.schifferbooks.com. You may also write for a free catalog.

Schiffer Publishing's titles are available at special discounts for bulk purchases for sales promotions or premiums. Special editions, including personalized covers, corporate imprints, and excerpts, can be created in large quantities for special needs. For more information, contact the publisher.

We are always looking for people to write books on new and related subjects. If you have an idea for a book, please contact us at proposals@schifferbooks.com.

First designed and published in Japan in 2020 by Graphic-sha Publishing Co., Ltd.
© 2020 Graphic-sha Publishing Co., Ltd.
English edition published in the United States of America in 2023 by Schiffer Publishing, Ltd.

Original edition creative staff
Editor/Writer: Hiroshi Sato
Photographer: Kazushige Takashima (Colors)
Design: Hiroaki Shiota
Cooperation: Daichi Takemoto, Kazumi Sato, Naoto Shirahata, Shu Asaoka, Susumu Yamaguchi, Takahisa Fujimoto, Takumi Kidokoro
Editor: Akira Sakamoto (Graphic-sha Publishing)

English edition creative staff
English translation: Kevin Wilson
English edition layout: Shinichi Ishioka
English edition production and management: Takako Motoki (Graphic-sha Publishing)